W9-BYH-083

University of Massachusetts Amherst

THE CAMPUS GUIDE

University of Massachusetts Amherst

AN ARCHITECTURAL TOUR BY
Marla R. Miller and Max Page

FOREWORD BY
Kumble R. Subbaswamy

PRINCETON ARCHITECTURAL PRESS
NEW YORK

Published by

Princeton Architectural Press

37 East Seventh Street

New York, New York 10003

Visit our website at www.papress.com.

© 2013 Princeton Architectural Press

All rights reserved

Printed and bound in China

16 15 14 13 4 3 2 1 First edition

No part of this book may be used or reproduced in any manner without written permission from the publisher, except in the context of reviews.

Every reasonable attempt has been made to identify owners of copyright. Errors or omissions will be corrected in subsequent editions.

Series Editor: Jan Hartman

PAPress Editor: Dan Simon

Layout: Benjamin English

Mapmaker: Tom Gastel

Special thanks to: Sara Bader, Janet Behning, Nicola Bednarek Brower, Fannie Bushin, Megan Carey, Carina Cha, Andrea Chlad, Russell Fernandez, Will Foster, Jan Haux, Diane Levinson, Jennifer Lippert, Jacob Moore, Katharine Myers, Margaret Rogalski, Elana Schlenker, Sara Stemen, Andrew Stepanian, Paul Wagner, and Joseph Weston of Princeton Architectural Press —Kevin C. Lippert, publisher

Library of Congress Cataloging-in-Publication Data

University of Massachusetts Amherst: an architectural tour / by Marla R. Miller and Max Page; foreword by Kumble R. Subbaswamy. — 1st ed.

p. cm. — (The campus guide)

Includes bibliographical references and index.

ISBN 978-1-61689-112-1 (pbk.: alk. paper)

1. University of Massachusetts Amherst—Buildings. 2. University of Massachusetts Amherst—History. I. Title.

LD3234.M234M55 2013

378.744'23—dc23

2012019594

Contents

How to Use This Guide

We hope this book will be used by visitors, alumni, staff, faculty, and students who are eager to learn more about the three centuries of architecture and landscapes that constitute the University of Massachusetts Amherst. The story of this 150-year-old public university is written into the buildings and grounds of the campus.

The guide opens with an introduction that lays out the history of the university with particular attention to the series of landmark campus plans, beginning with the vision submitted by none other than celebrated landscape architect Frederick Law Olmsted (and promptly set aside by the school's founders). We then offer five Walks that touch on every part of the campus, encompassing dozens of buildings, landscapes, artworks, and memorials. Each Walk begins with a brief overview of the central themes and events that have shaped that section of campus, and each building is illustrated and discussed, with emphasis given to how the building reflects the evolving history of this public university. We take special pride in focusing on the works of some of the most important twentieth-century architects who have built or made plans for UMass: Kevin Roche; Edward Durrell Stone; Marcel Breuer; Skidmore, Owings & Merrill; and Sasaki Associates. Many of the Walks begin and/or end at the university's traditional gathering spaces—the University Club, the Student Union, the Lincoln Campus Center, the Gunness Engineering Student Center, and the Robsham Visitor's Center—inviting users on the ground in Amherst to pause to enjoy those spaces at more leisure. A beautiful watercolor map identifies the sites on each Walk.

Whether you live or work here, have attended the university, or are contemplating doing so, we hope that you will use this guide not only to explore the distinctive architectural legacy of the campus, but also to discover our unique history.

VISITORS TO UMASS ARE MORE THAN WELCOME:
Please visit www.umass.edu to learn more about the university.
For campus tours, contact or visit the Robsham Memorial Center for Visitors:
300 Massachusetts Avenue, Amherst, MA 01003; phone: 413-545-0306.

Lederle Graduate Research Building, the W. E. B. Du Bois Library, the Southwest Residential Area: If you approach our campus from the west, these towers boldly announce one's arrival at the University of Massachusetts Amherst. If you come in the afternoon, when the light is just right, you are treated to the play of the sun and shadows off these majestic buildings. For the truly fortunate, the light show is accompanied by the sounds of the Minuteman Marching Band as they practice on a crisp autumn afternoon next to the Mullins Center. And if you are familiar with the university as a student, alumnus, or employee, it is at that moment that you know that you are *home*.

The architecture of our campus does more than alert those who approach that they have arrived at UMass Amherst—although it does this dramatically well. It also tells us that ours is a particular and special kind of university, one devoted to both *excellence* and *access*. Lederle, after all, houses scientists committed to excellence in research, and indeed it is named for the person, President John Lederle, most associated with the promotion of research and discovery at UMass Amherst. The W. E. B. Du Bois Library, an impressive repository of knowledge and site of student interaction, pays homage to a native son who fought for racial equality and justice. Finally, the towers of the Southwest Residential Area, as if to make a point both geographically and metaphorically, announce our mission to educate and house not just a narrow few, but all the citizens of the Commonwealth of Massachusetts. Together these three complexes, perhaps more than any other buildings on campus, demonstrate who we are and what we do.

Two building booms mark our history over the last seventy or so years. The first accompanied the democratization and expansion of public higher education

The Fine Arts Center at the top of Haigis Mall today

in Massachusetts, and it produced the very buildings mentioned thus far. The second is underway currently and has produced within the last few years significant additions to the campus such as the Studio Arts Building, the Integrated Science Building, the New Laboratory Science Building, the Recreation Center, the George N. Parks Marching Band Building, and the Commonwealth Honors College Complex. As this book went to press the Academic Classroom Building was rising in the heart of the campus, and landscaping associated with the Campus Master Plan, adopted recently, brings a new order and beauty to the entire university.

This feast or famine history of construction means that the campus looks very familiar to some and less so to others, depending on when one attended UMass. Graduates from before World War II returning to campus encountered a very different place in the 1970s. In turn, graduates from the 1970s returning to campus today encounter a dramatically different built environment than they experienced as students. This is the nature of UMass Amherst as it grows and evolves to best fulfill its mission of education and access. For this reason the *University of Massachusetts Amherst* Campus Guide is especially welcome, as it will reintroduce and explain the campus to many, even as it introduces newcomers to our architectural past and present. The Guide will, in short, welcome all of us home to this place we love so well.

Go UMass!
Dr. Kumble R. Subbaswamy
Chancellor of the University of Massachusetts Amherst

I have long believed that I became interested in architecture by walking up a ramp from the dank underbelly of the stadium and out into the surreal light and primal roar of that emerald jewel, Fenway Park.

But I realize now that I first truly began to think about architecture from watching this brave new campus rise from a collection of nineteenth-century agricultural college structures.

I am part of a very small alumni category: UMass faculty who are children of former UMass faculty. My father, Alex Page, taught in the English Department for thirty years. He told my brother and me stories about when he first arrived at the university—or, more precisely, what had until recently been called Massachusetts Agricultural College—in the 1950s, as it was about to explode into a major research university. His department shared the Old Chapel with the math and music departments. The football stadium—well, "field"—stood where the Whitmore Administration Building now stands.

I didn't go to UMass (although I did take my first college classes here), but I felt like I was immersed in the University's life from the start of my life, spending my first year on Fearing Street, across fields where cows once grazed and where Southwest would stand. Growing up in the late 1960s and early '70s, I was awed by the sheer weight of the new buildings, especially Southwest, the Fine Arts Center, and the Du Bois library—the tallest in the world when first built, as we proudly bragged everywhere we went. As a young boy, inseparable from his bike, I spun around these buildings, down the ramps, coasting from Whitmore all the way down Hicks Way to the library, appreciating (without having words for it) their sculptural quality and the sense that here was something new, something so different from what I saw when I went sledding down Memorial Hill at Amherst College.

What I want to suggest is that the architecture of this campus, far from being impersonal, cold, and drab, as some say, was in fact a heroic statement of the value of a public university. As the college became a university with aspirations to turn Massachusetts citizens into national leaders in the second half of the twentieth century, it chose not to mimic the colleges nearby—brick Amherst College, Gothic Mt. Holyoke, Victorian Smith. No, UMass's leaders decided that this national public research university would stake its claim as something modern through its architecture. This university would be elite but not elitist, it would be open and accessible, and it would pursue research in the

Max Page, age ten, at the new Fine Arts Center, overlooking the Campus Center

public interest. There was to be nothing quaint or precious about this new university. It would unshakably place itself as herald of the future.

UMass is in pursuit of a long-delayed goal of joining the ranks of the very finest public research universities. It will be important, as we pursue that goal, not to sever ties to what has defined us in the past. Our uniqueness is symbolized in our architecture—the early buildings of this significant agricultural college that are our roots, and the thrilling, weighty buildings of concrete that marked UMass in the last half of the twentieth century. To paraphrase what Alain de Botton wrote in *The Architecture of Happiness*: we should be sure, as we embark on this physical and institutional building process, that what we build is worthy of the founders of the agricultural college in the nineteenth century, and the visionary leaders who remade it in the mid-twentieth.

This preface is adapted from "Preserving the Future," *UMass Alumni Magazine* (Fall 2008) http://umassmag.com/2008/Fall_2008/features/building.html.

The North and Northwest complexes

My first glimpse of the UMass campus was from the top of Mt. Sugarloaf, a state reservation area in South Deerfield, Massachusetts, about eleven miles north of campus. I was then a junior at the University of Wisconsin-Madison and had just arrived in Historic Deerfield, where I was attending their Summer Fellowship Program in early American history and culture. The program director, Kevin Sweeney (now a professor of history at Amherst College), brought us to the top of Sugarloaf, the southern terminus of the Pocumtuck Range, so that we could take in that iconic view of the broad river heading south toward the Holyoke Range. From Sugarloaf we could see the remnants of seventeenth-century land-use patterns and appreciate the ways that towns were laid out around meeting-houses and encircled by fields and woodlands.

Standing on the observation platform, I could see a series of towers rising in the distance. "What's that city over there?" I asked. People laughed, and I was embarrassed, feeling every bit the fish out of water that I was in the earliest days of that summer.

The program was a life-changing experience. I couldn't have guessed then that a dozen years later I would land a job on that very campus, moving into an office amid the immense concrete coffers of Herter Hall. Having been drawn to the Valley by its spectacular scenery and rich eighteenth-century history, I didn't give much thought to the design of the building I was in. Like most of my colleagues and students, I cringed slightly at the chaotic nature of the built environment.

In time, however, my perceptions changed. I married and moved into a house built in 1956, prompting new curiosity about the culture that cultivated the mid-century modern aesthetic, interest that grew as I searched for furniture, lighting, and housewares sympathetic to our home's era while the popularity of *Mad Men* fueled nationwide interest in all things retro. I taught an undergraduate seminar on American material culture in a room in Herter Hall, and, in a pinch for an artifact that the class could examine hands-on, launched a study of the (fascinating) Emeco 501, the wonderful postwar upholstered aluminum chairs still scattered around the building's halls. Most importantly, I was fascinated by the work that one of our students, Jayne Bernhard Armington, completed in a class with my colleague Max Page.

Through Jayne's draft of a proposed nomination for Herter Hall to the National Register of Historic Places, I saw the building with fresh eyes. Suddenly the concrete, the grid, the windows, and other things that we had chuckled about made sense to me. My appreciation for not only that building but also others—Marcel Breuer's bewitching campus center, Kevin Roche's iconic Fine Arts Center—grew. I was converted. I began to see small moments of delight everywhere. When I stumbled upon the campus center's wonderful parking structure featured in the National Building Museum's exhibition House of Cars: Innovation and the Parking Garage, I was delighted but not surprised in the least.

The towers of the UMass campus (left, in distance), as seen from the top of Mt. Sugarloaf

This book emerged out of a desire to share those epiphanies with others. Every day the students, faculty, and staff who work at UMass pass through a built environment that is unique and fascinating. This project aims to impart to new readers the utter delight Jayne helped me find in the buildings and landscapes we experience every day—to appreciate the way light pierces through the lattice walls of the parking garage, how the tessellations of Herter and Tobin halls are answered in those of the Campus Center, the ways the

steeply pitched red-brick gables of South College are reflected and renewed
in the design of the newest residential area. Understood in their various con-
texts, the buildings that together make up the UMass campus are all artifacts
of times, places, and people that open insight into the special history of this
place. As pleased as I am to draw your attention to the architectural moments
that most delight my own sensibilities, I hope that these pages help you to
find your own.

BEAUTY, CRAVINGS, AND VIRTUE

Alain de Botton, philosopher and author of *The Architecture of Happiness*, has written:

> We are drawn to call something beautiful whenever we detect that it contains in a concentrated form those qualities in which we personally, or our societies more generally, are deficient. We respect a style which can move us away from what we fear towards what we crave; a style which carries the correct dosage of our missing virtues.[1]

Beautiful has not always been the word attached to the architecture of the University of Massachusetts. Our goal in this guidebook is to do nothing less than use that word proudly for the Amherst campus. We find individual buildings and landscapes beautiful, but also the century-and-a-half quest to provide higher education for the Commonwealth's citizens.

To be sure, the appeal of the campus is not in its uniformity of vision and completeness of design. Visitors will not confuse this place with Stanford University, whose core Romanesque and Spanish Mission–inspired buildings were constructed within a few short years, or Yale's Gothic colleges, built all at once in the midst of the Depression. Founded in a state with more private colleges than any other in the union, the University of Massachusetts has been engaged in a long debate in brick and steel and lots of concrete about the appropriate image for a major public university. The campus, both its glorious buildings and its less-beloved ones, is part of a noble story—perhaps the most noble story we have—of the attempt to achieve the vision Governor John A. Andrew announced to the legislature on January 9, 1863: "We should have a university which would be worthy of the dream of her fathers, the history of the state, and the capacity of her people."[2] The University of Massachusetts has spent the last 150 years trying to figure out what it means to be a public institution of higher education. As the university celebrates the beginning of its next 150 years, it will continue to ask what our buildings should say to the Commonwealth and to the nation.

There are a number of story lines here, in what has been at times nothing short of a tragicomedy. First is the interplay between the rural setting and agricultural origins of the original campus and the sophistication of a modern research institution. This is a campus of contrasts, from Southwest's high-rise dormitories to Prexy's Ridge and its old-growth forest, and the 400-acre Waugh Arboretum, which covers a good portion of the campus. From the top of the tallest building here you look down upon fields not a quarter mile away that have been cultivated for more than three and a half centuries. In the shadow of cutting-edge research that may one day lead to bacteria-powered

Inside the Durfee Conservatory

The Durfee Plant House and other early campus buildings, looking west toward Hadley, circa 1880

appliances is the Stockbridge House (1728) where farmers once debated the American Revolution and a budding artist named Daniel Chester French first started sketching—on the walls of his home.

These contrasts speak to another central theme of our story: dramatic change. When the college opened its doors in 1867, there were four faculty members and fifty-six students; the population today stands at about 28,000 graduate and undergraduate students. It may have taken several years after the establishment of the school in 1863 to build its first building, but a century later only two of the original buildings still survived, and they too would soon fall. The campus has gone through the ups and downs of the economy and state funding, shifting ideas of its multiple missions, and changes in organization.

The most dramatic metamorphosis came after World War II with the second-most important act in public higher education's history (the first being the Morrill Act of 1862, discussed below): the passage of the GI Bill (officially called the Servicemen's Readjustment Act) of 1944, which gave millions of returning veterans and their children the opportunity to attend college. The population of college students soon tripled and the number of public research universities quintupled (from 25 to 125) in a mere two decades. UMass was, therefore, building to accommodate the tidal wave of students while also trying to establish itself in a community of national research institutions.

Finally, there is the question of appreciation. It would be dishonest for us—UMass faculty with an open affection for our university and its campus—to fail to acknowledge that many others disagree. Not long ago at least one online source conferred on UMass Amherst the dubious distinction of being the second ugliest campus in the nation (with Drexel University in Philadelphia named the "winner"). As we began our research, the director of student affairs declared the architecture of the Southwest Residential Area to be "brutal." Art students have long complained about the leaks in the Fine Arts Center. And this is not a new feeling. Robert Campbell, architecture critic for the *Boston Globe*, wrote in 1974 that the campus is "a jumble of unrelated personal monuments that looks more like a world fairgrounds than a campus."[3]

Of course, much the same was said of New York brownstones, beloved in the nineteenth century, hated in the early twentieth, and cherished again toward the end of the millennium. Or the red-brick homes of Boston, swept aside in the 1950s to make way for the modern era. Every style has had its day, and usually more than one. Beauty is indeed in the eye of the beholder. But the beholder's eye changes over time, and what was once ugly can become beautiful—just as it may become ugly once again. For every observer who believes that "these power-fully shaped buildings have great visual interest—especially in a strong sun that shows off their crisp edges, stripped surfaces and Brobdingnagian geometry," there is another who finds them "drab and uninviting."[4]

The reactions to this architectural landscape could make for an interesting study in and of itself; the themes that flow through the urban legends surround-ing many of these buildings (subjects we tackle in this guide) are telling for the assumptions they reveal about the history of this place. Stories of malfunction-ing structures (falling bricks, mislaid steam pipes) often hinge on notions of bungling managers who failed to foresee obvious physical challenges, if not impossibilities, while narratives of second-rate or off-the-shelf plans compete with others about arrogant architects unwilling to compromise their aesthetic vision or condescend to practicality. The voices we found in the university archives confirmed none of the urban legends repeated so often around campus; instead, we saw how each of these structures reflects complex long-term negotia-tions among an array of disparate interests and concerns. How one assesses the outcomes of those negotiations aside, the process itself was rarely a simple one.

Whatever the opinion, one thing is clear: the UMass campus hosts examples of significant works of architecture by some of the most important architects and architectural firms of their time. The campus boasts three centuries of American buildings and landscapes. As Arnold Friedmann, longtime historian of the cam-pus buildings, has said, "It is a bit like a dictionary of architecture."[5] Architects Kevin Roche, Edward Durrell Stone, Marcel Breuer, Hugh Stubbins, Skidmore, Owings & Merrill, Graham Gund, William Rawn, Cambridge 7, Campbell and Aldrich, and planners and landscape designers Frederick Law Olmsted, Warren H. Manning, Frank Waugh, and Sasaki Associates have all left their imprint on the campus, which also contains the most extensive work of important regional architects such as Louis Warren Ross and James H. Ritchie. Alain de Botton wrote that "clashes of taste are an inevitable by-product of a world where forces continually fragment and deplete us in new ways.... As the ways in which are unbalanced alters, so our attention will continue to be drawn to new parts of the spectrum of taste, to new styles which we will declare beautiful on the basis

that they embody in a concentrated form what now lies in shadow within us."[6]
His words raise the question: why now do we and many others have new appreciation for the buildings of UMass, especially its modern buildings of the past fifty years? In an age when the very idea of public institutions has been under attack, many have gained a new appreciation of the monuments built at the height of faith in government. We have looked past the chips that once fell from upper-story bricks and out-of-service elevators to stand in awe at the idealism of building the world's tallest library, open to anyone, twenty-four hours a day. We have found ourselves willing to forgive the cracks in the concrete of the Fine Arts Center because we are moved by the decision to ask one of the premier architects of the day to design first-class art, music, and theater spaces for the sons and daughters of working men and women of Massachusetts. We lament that the state hasn't been consistent, to say the least, in its commitment to maintain its flagship campus, but we still take pride in the extraordinary constellation of landscapes and buildings that attest to the continued mission of the university.

We hope that after taking these Walks, what had once seemed like a jumble of things that don't make sense will be more legible as the revealing product of this ongoing conversation about the nature and value of a public university. That is a conversation worth having, and a reason to celebrate the University of Massachusetts campus. We hope that after taking some of these tours you will appreciate our architectural heritage. But even if we can't convince you to love a twenty-eight-story library, or if concrete just isn't your thing, we hope you will recognize what the builders of this campus had in mind: a national, public research university worthy of the Commonwealth, and one that contributes to the scientific and cultural advancement of the state and the nation.

FOUNDING A COLLEGE

The University of Massachusetts Amherst may have had its own dramatic history, but it rests on the solid remains of an epic revolution of another kind. The history of the University and its built environment cannot be disentangled from longer geologic stories. Volcanic activity millions of years ago created the landmass now called the Holyoke Range—hills that remember when they were mountains, in the words of a local singer-songwriter. The advance and retreat of a large glacier in the centuries to follow created drumlins and kettle holes that still define the modern campus. The sculptural lines of the Range today create a signature silhouette that continues to define the southern horizon, both for the UMass campus and for Amherst College nearby. About 18,000 years ago, glacial meltwaters, unable to pass large deposits at what is now Rocky Hill, Connecticut, created a 140-mile lake that extended north to St. Johnsbury, Vermont. In time, the dam yielded; as the lake drained, the Connecticut River as we know it now took shape (and a scenic shape it was: the Connecticut River, today one of just fourteen American Heritage Rivers in the United States, was featured in Thomas Cole's celebrated masterpiece, *View from Mount Holyoke*...

The tops of the Holyoke Range define the southern horizon

after a Thunderstorm—*The Oxbow* (1836), which helped launch the Hudson River School of landscape painting and has become one of the most reproduced images of the nineteenth century). As a channel settled beneath the lake, fertile and easy to till terraces emerged. The campus rests on this series of terraces, from the ridge on the east created by the glacier that carved its way from the north (we now call this Orchard Hill) to a glacial lake bed to the west where the town of Hadley now sits.

The rich alluvial farmland left by the millions of years of melting ice attracted a succession of populations, including the Norwottuck people and, in time, the English migrants who coveted this productive farmland. European settlement made its way up the valley from Connecticut beginning in the 1630s. In 1661 the town of Hadley was incorporated, and, in 1759, its eastern precinct was set off as a separate town named for Lord Jeffrey Amherst, who had recently seen success in Britain's ongoing effort to eject France from North America. Eighteenth-century residents concentrated on raising cattle; nineteenth-century farmers planted broom corn, a crop later succeeded by tobacco, onions, squash, and asparagus.

The contemporary campus consists of some 1,400 acres, about two-thirds of which fall within the town of Amherst, with the balance in the neighboring town of Hadley. Orchard Hill bounds our eastern edge, and the Mill River the western, while Wildwood Brook defines the north end. The town of Amherst lies to the south, the spires of its several churches visible from the top of the eleven-story Campus Center. To the west are Mount Warner and the Connecticut River, with the foothills of the Berkshires beyond. The Green Mountains rise to the north, the Pelham Hills to the east, all visible across broad expanses of farmland.

The historian Marc Bloch despaired of the "idol of origins," our obsession with finding an exact date when something began.[7] We have one of those origin dates for the University of Massachusetts; it is April 29, 1863, when the General Court of Massachusetts (the state legislature) voted to create the Massachusetts Agricultural College. It is a legitimate birthday that is celebrated annually. But Bloch was right to despair, because marking one date alone brushes aside a lot of history. While we place the founding of the Massachusetts Agricultural College in 1863 (the school that eventually became the Massachusetts State College in 1931 and then the University of Massachusetts in 1947), the movement for a public university accessible to the masses began long before. At the same time, efforts to think more systematically about agriculture and to disseminate insights more widely had been afoot for decades before the Morrill Act made this institution possible. The building of the campus where those trends entwine has been a continuing work in progress ever since.

Massachusetts's first publicly funded college—yes, Harvard—was established in 1636 but had become steadily more private and exclusive. Horace Mann pioneered universal public education in Massachusetts and inaugurated the first teachers' colleges in the early 1800s. Given the centrality of agriculture to the local economy, it is not surprising that efforts to improve production appeared early on in the state. Among the earliest agricultural societies in the United States, the Massachusetts Society for Promoting Agriculture (MSPA), incorporated in 1792 (and still in existence), aimed to encourage research that would improve agricultural technologies and practices. The MSPA later took an early interest in the new agricultural college and continues to provide scholarships for students and contributions to the work of the research facilities.

Elsewhere, agricultural schools had been developed in the 1830s to provide practical training for farmers. In 1856 a group of farmers in North Hadley collectively declared that "the interest of Agriculture would be materially promoted by the formation of a farmers club."[8] The organization's founding secretary, 36-year-old Levi Stockbridge (an ambitious farmer, and later president of the college), recorded discussions of everything from how to apply manure to the moral implications of tobacco farming.

Amateur pomologist Marshall P. Wilder (like Stockbridge, an energetic entrepreneur and joiner) is today credited with being the first advocate of a Massachusetts Agricultural College. A founder or president of the Massachusetts Horticultural Society (1829), the American Pomological Society (1848), the United States Agricultural Society (1852), and the New England Historic Genealogical Society in the 1840s, Wilder was a born institution-builder. As a founding member of the State Board of Agriculture in 1852, he found a venue in which to advance the cause of formal agricultural education.

The 1862 federal Morrill Act made the dream a reality by providing that indispensable partner to dreams: money. One of the most important pieces of legislation in American history, the Morrill Act (named after Vermont representative Justin S. Morrill) was signed by Abraham Lincoln to promote the "liberal and practical education of the industrial classes for the benefit of Agricultural and Mechanic Arts." It gave land in the American West to each state in proportion to the number of members of Congress it had. Massachusetts was allotted 360,000 acres, which it sold for $29,778.40 to support the recently established Massachusetts Institute of Technology (MIT) and create an endowment for the Massachusetts Agricultural College (MAC). Iowa would be the first state to found such a school, but Massachusetts soon followed.

The money assured the decision to finally build an agricultural college but did not determine where it would be. Indeed, it was hardly a foregone conclusion that a new agricultural college would be owned and funded by the state. Many under the "golden dome" (that is, the Massachusetts State House on Boston's Beacon Hill) thought an agricultural college should simply be a subsidiary of Harvard's Bussey Institute. Advocates in the town of Amherst thought that perhaps the new agricultural college should be a part of their now nearly fifty-year-old private college; many of the key proponents of bringing the agricultural college to western Massachusetts were Amherst College faculty. Other towns competed as well. Northampton briefly contemplated a school, and Springfield had come within a few votes in the legislature of gaining a state agricultural college fifteen years before the passage of the Morrill Act. But Stockbridge and the membership of the Hampshire County Agricultural Society—including Amherst College professor William Smith Clark—would prove influential: indeed, Stockbridge and Clark both served on the State Board of Agriculture, and in 1864 were members of the state House of Representatives, and so were well positioned to steer the course of these events.

In the end it was a unique public-private partnership that would seal the deal for Amherst. When a town meeting authorized spending $50,000 of their citizens' money and when leaders from Amherst College agreed to contribute to the cause, the day was won. In 1864 six farms were purchased to form the new Massachusetts Agricultural College. "Who can estimate the importance of having, in the midst of an agricultural community, a model farm of four hundred acres," declared the trustees, "where model farm-buildings, implements, domestic animals, orchards, field crops and garden, and all the processes of the most enlightened agriculture, are continually upon exhibition. The College will also furnish a superior education, of an eminently practical character, to the young men of Amherst, either gratis or at a very small expense."[9]

BUILDING THE CAMPUS
It is fair to say that UMass had a profound influence on dozens of other land-grant campuses. But not in the most flattering way. In 1864 the trustees hired Frederick Law Olmsted's collaborator on Manhattan's Central Park, Calvert Vaux, to suggest a plan for the first buildings. Less than pleased with the plan (which imagined the campus arranged around a single main building high up on the ridge where Butterfield Hall and the Clark Memorial now stand), the new board of trustees asked Olmsted himself to weigh in. Olmsted went beyond

his charge, and in 1866 the famed landscape architect wrote to the trustees with his thoughts on the ideal plans for agricultural colleges. He rejected the typical approach of a large multiuse building in an open landscape. Olmsted recommended instead a campus plan that reflected the layout of a New England village, with a series of small buildings clustered relatively close together on the eastern slope of the college's property, and built as needed by the growing institution.

The trustees, having lured a famous local (Olmsted was born some 55 miles south, in Hartford, Connecticut) into this discussion, promptly ignored most of his advice and sent him on his way. Contrary to Olmsted's advice, the trustees did what previous colleges had done: build a single grand building (or in this case, two: South and North College) to house dormitories, offices, and laboratories. Against the recommendations of both Olmsted and Vaux, they set UMass's version of the "Old Main" building on other college campuses on the western ridge. And so UMass, more recently known as a bastion of liberal activism, began its history with a conservative gesture. Olmsted, as it happens, had better luck across town. Amherst College, which had borrowed Yale's model of a line of buildings facing the community, took Olmsted's advice and, as it grew, chose to turn inward, creating its own academic quadrangle.

Two significant recommendations by Olmsted were, however, implemented and remain central elements of the campus landscape. Over the next thirty years, a long road, curving from North Pleasant Street over to the western ridge and back to North Pleasant, was named after Olmsted. Olmsted Way defined the pathway of the campus and became the spine along which later buildings were constructed. Olmsted also suggested that the marshy lowlands between the two ridges be turned into a pond. The Campus Pond was not built until the turn of the twentieth century, but it quickly became the physical and emotional center of campus.

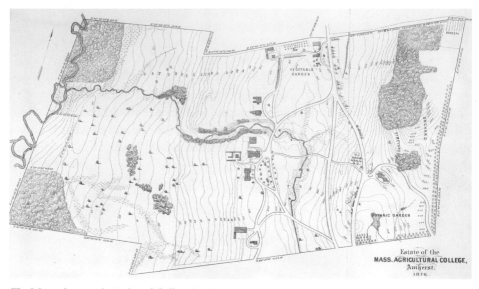

The Massachusetts Agricultural College in 1870

But these developments came well into the future. Feeling his expertise was ignored, Olmsted announced his displeasure. He published a version of his report to the trustees, "How Not to Establish an Agricultural College," in *The Nation*: "In the midst of an open agricultural country, where no one can suppose abundant ground space difficult to obtain," he wrote, "a straight-sided, evenly-balanced, many-storied structure of stone, will not be merely incongruous to the landscape, but will certainly impose quite unnecessary inconvenience and fatigue upon those who are to occupy it." [10] Instead, he argued that "you must embrace in your ground-plan arrangements for something more than oral instruction and practical demonstration in the science of agriculture, and for the practice of various rural arts. You must include arrangements designed to favorably affect the habits and inclinations of your students, and to qualify them for a wise and beneficent exercise of the rights and duties of citizens and of householders." [11] In essence, he argued for the creation of a community, with education as its mission, as opposed to an educational institution alone. This vision, and the planning ideas animating it, caught the attention of other new land-grant colleges and beginning in 1867 Olmsted was awarded the job of planning several other land-grant colleges along this villagelike approach.

It was one of Olmsted's students and employees, Warren H. Manning, who in the 1910s took a second try at bringing Olmsted's vision to the campus. Manning, a key figure in the rise of landscape architecture as a profession and a voice in the creation of the national parks, was hired and retained for four years to produce and implement a plan for a campus that had grown in size and vision. Despite the rise and fall in state financial support (including cyclical calls by some for the state to shed this costly endeavor altogether), the campus expanded in numbers of students and diversity of buildings. A dozen new buildings had been completed and the curriculum had expanded beyond the traditional agricultural subjects.

A new plan was needed. Manning later wrote that in developing his vision he went back to the studies of Vaux and the "very important report and plan" of Olmsted. He sought to bring order to growth by creating not the single academic village Olmsted had originally proposed, but three, according to the different activities of the growing college. Horticultural service would be in the Upland Section; research, administration, and science would be in the Midland around the campus pond and a new pond (on the site of what is now the Campus Center); finally, the Lowland Section would house farm buildings for animals. The bulk of the buildings were grouped relatively close together, and labs, classrooms, and residence halls were placed near to their schools' fields and farm buildings.

In developing and implementing the plan, he relied on Frank Waugh, author of the classic *Book of Landscape Gardening* (1899) and head of the new Department of Landscape Gardening established in 1903—just the second program of its kind in the United States. As a teacher, Waugh advised students to

The center of campus in the 1920s

improve their understanding of landscape forms by studying Corot; he played his flute alongside a rushing stream to cultivate an appreciation for the landscape aural qualities. Waugh also shaped the landscapes of the U.S. National Park System (including that of Grand Canyon Village) at the invitation of his former student Conrad Wirth, NPS director (1951–64) and a UMass alumnus, and consulted with the U.S. Forest Service as well, becoming a nationally recognized landscape architect.

Waugh and Manning shared a vision of a campus where the designed landscapes and buildings would blend in with the natural setting. Inspired by Olmsted's original vision for the campus, Waugh strove to integrate academic pursuits and the natural, rural setting. As Wirth would later recall, Waugh "proceeded on the principle that man's advanced culture and social development required certain modern conveniences but that these utilities should not be ugly or destructive of the natural environment."[12] Waugh would even suggest that the campus meadow be maintained by a flock of sheep, "adding to the idyllic quality of campus."[13]

Although Manning began working at the College when there were fewer than 500 students, and could hardly imagine the 28,000 students who would attend the University by the end of the century, his plan, implemented over two decades, had a lasting influence. As you walk the campus today, you still see the clusters of science buildings at the north end of campus, the strong central core around the campus pond, and the sprawling farm and athletic buildings heading down the western slope to the plain.

Through the 1920s, the campus remained a quiet, open landscape of dispersed buildings. But with the transition of the agricultural college to a more general state college in 1931, and especially to a university in 1947, came explosive changes.

Plymouth Dorm in the so-called County Circle, October 1951

Pressure from students and alumni through the 1920s eventually led MAC's trustees to support a transition to the Massachusetts State College; on March 26, 1931, Governor Joseph B. Ely signed a measure effecting the change of name, but lacking any discussion that would redefine the institution's purpose. But that purpose nevertheless slowly began to evolve away from a purely agricultural and technical focus to a broader liberal arts curriculum.

World War II would prove to be a watershed; from then until the mid-1980s, enrollment expanded at an average rate of nearly six hundred additional students every year for forty years. Over ten million square feet of space was built within twenty years to accommodate the new students and faculty. Where the Morrill Land Grant Act had created the public university system, it was the GI Bill that finally brought public higher education to the masses. Under pressure of returning veterans seeking a college education, the dream of a "University of Massachusetts"—first contemplated in the early nineteenth century—became a reality in 1947. New buildings, some slapdash and some well conceived, went up regularly in the years following. One of the defining features of the campus is that utilitarian buildings (such as the concrete-block buildings just south and east of Boyden Gym, each built in 1948 to house 150 individuals or thirty families) stand directly next to and underneath works by some of the finest architects of their time. Such was the rush of growth after World War II and especially from the 1950s through the 1970s.

With enrollment rapidly climbing beyond 4,000, the campus called on the firm of Schurcliff, Schurcliff & Merrill to help it thoughtfully build toward its future. The firm imagined a campus of 10,000 students, far more densely built up, that incorporated cars and their homes (that is, parking lots) into the plan.

But growth outpaced that vision, and only seven years later, yet another plan was needed. The 1962 Plan of Sasaki, Dawson, DeMay (later Sasaki Associates) did more than prepare for a seemingly unstoppable growth in the student population. It fundamentally reoriented UMass away from its agricultural roots to an urban campus form and set the stage for the modernist monuments that define the campus today. This transformation went hand in hand with the growing aspirations of the campus, which aimed to serve both as a training ground for students of the Commonwealth and as a research institution of national and international scope.

The key figure in this period was President Lederle, who led the campus during its era of greatest growth, 1960 to 1970. His goal was nothing less than to

President John Lederle with a copy of history professor Harold W. Cary's 1963 book The University of Massachusetts: A History of One Hundred Years

build "a great public center for excellence in higher education in this region," "advance the frontiers of knowledge," and "transmit knowledge."[14] "We have in the University of Massachusetts," he said, "a potential giant." Lederle was insistent that the broadening of opportunity for public higher education was "an inherent part of the democratic process." Under his leadership (as well as that of his much-admired provost, Oswald Tippo), both student enrollment and faculty ranks tripled. By 1972, students numbered over 23,000. In 1962, 1 of every 150 young Massachusetts adults was at UMass; by 1972 it was 1 of every 45. The University became a comprehensive research university and dramatically expanded its graduate school. Lederle also presided over the expansion of UMass to two other sites—the urban campus in Boston (1964) and the medical school in Worcester (1962).

To pave the way for a much larger campus with much larger ambitions, Hideo Sasaki moved dramatically away from the naturalistic campus of Manning and Waugh. First, he proposed moving most vehicular circulation to the edges of the campus, effectively creating a ring road around an ever-denser core. Olmsted / Ellis Way was finally removed (although it will be possible on tours of the campus to glimpse its imprint) and North Pleasant would be closed to vehicular traffic (an idea around since at least the 1950s and never implemented, but incorporated into the 2012 campus master plan). More importantly, he set the stage for the modernist icons that would be built over the course of the 1960s and early 1970s: the Southwest Residential Area, home to five thousand students; the massive Fine Arts Center complex; the Lincoln Campus Center; the so-called tower library; and the striking football stadium. During a single decade almost fifty buildings totaling over two million square feet rose, doubling the space on campus. Agricultural buildings were moved further and further to the periphery. Indeed, many of the original agricultural activities of the university now take place many miles away—in Hadley, South Deerfield, and Belchertown.

Sasaki did not design any new buildings, but he called on the university to hire an architectural consultant to select visionaries to design signature buildings in the new plan. Sasaki and the university's choice was Pietro Belluschi,

This image from the Sasaki plan is more artful than it is descriptive, but shows the vision that redefined this landscape in the 1960s.

a key figure in the modernist movement. Dean of the MIT School of Architecture, Belluschi guided several campus planning projects in these years. It was he who advised the university to hire Kevin Roche, Gordon Bunshaft, Marcel Breuer, and Edward Durrell Stone. While Sasaki and Belluschi embraced modernism, they did not seek uniformity for the campus. Far more important to them was to build shelters for the students, faculty, research, and teaching of the booming university, and to project an image of a forward-looking institution ready to take its place among the leading universities in the nation.

A class convenes outside the newly built Herter Hall.

The Southwest Residential Area

Even as it looked to model itself on institutions around the country, UMass came into a closer relationship with its neighboring colleges. In 1965 UMass joined the newly formed consortium Five Colleges, Inc., which unites Amherst and Hampshire colleges in Amherst, Mount Holyoke College in South Hadley, and Smith College in Northampton in an academic and administrative collaboration. Many of the architects who contributed buildings to the UMass campus would work with the other colleges as well, and we make special note of those architects whose work spans the area colleges.

The result of these labors was met at the outset with enthusiasm, at least from the wider world. *Architectural Record* devoted a sizeable section of its May 1966 issue to a survey of the "Distinguished Architecture for a State University."[15] Calling the UMass approach a model for all colleges and universities undergoing expansion, the issue praised Hugh Stubbins's vision for the Southwest dormitories as "masterful"; the combination of high- and low-rises were "powerfully shaped buildings" that "proclaim that the University of Massachusetts is getting some architecture and knows where to put it." Meanwhile the "sculptured earth planes" at the base of the Campus Center cleverly enclose the space concealed below grade while preserving "an unimpeded view southward across the college pond toward the magnificent facade of Kevin Roche's Fine Arts Building," reaching toward the "broad terraces" that Roche envisioned on the south, which themselves reach back across the pond, visually linking the two landmark structures.

The years to follow witnessed what many now consider a defining era for the University of Massachusetts—the years in which student activism gave the campus the distinctive profile that it claims proudly today. The landscape that emerged in these years emerged from the confluence of many forces. Robert C. Wood, at his December 1970 installation as the seventeenth president of the university, reflecting on the tumultuous year that had seen extraordinary campus unrest nationwide (and, as we shall see, at UMass as well), noted that "it is open season on established mores, and the sacred cows of the campus—including university presidents," who "are being served up regularly for lunch." "Higher

The spire of Arnold House against the tower of the Lederle Graduate Research Center

education," he observed, "is being asked to defend its processes, its standards, its entire rationale." "I think, and the trustees think," he continued, that "the time has come to undertake more systematic changes. How do we build the public university of the future and not the public university of the '50s? What should the future university teach? How should we organize the university and its resources? What should it look like?"

"These are the questions that intrigue and trouble me, the trustees, the chancellors and the deans," Wood said, noting the centrality of architecture to the discussion: "Each month we are asked to review the plans for another carefully designed building...destined to be part of our scene for fifty years or more....If we don't try consciously to shape the University's future, the pressures of growth will shape it for us." "It is my conviction," Wood concluded, "that new patterns, new models must be found for University education in the Commonwealth."[16]

THE CAMPUS TODAY

The story of the UMass campus since the mid-1970s has been a three-part symphony: building, neglect, building. The massive expansion of the 1960s and 1970s was matched by two decades of relative disinvestment, and then a renewed construction program at the end of the century. Since the middle of the 1990s and especially in the first decade of the current millennium, UMass has been in a building boom only matched by the Lederle era, when the image of the campus was remade. "New Dirt" was the slogan and priority of Chancellor John Lombardi (2002–07), a "campus symbol for the creation of the new facilities for students and faculty that are required of a major national research university," and the phrase has stuck.[17] As the old made way for the new, in October 2007 Preservation Massachusetts, a statewide nonprofit organization dedicated to stewarding the Commonwealth's historic and cultural heritage, named the UMass Amherst campus one of the Bay State's "10 Most Endangered Historic Resources." Tension between past and present, heritage and innovation, continues to shape this landscape.

From a moment of especially acute strain emerged Preserve UMass, an organization of former and current University of Massachusetts Amherst professors, staff, and alumni. A watchdog group that arose after it appeared that the university had not followed proper procedures in demolishing the early-twentieth-century barn that stood in the way of the new Recreation Center, Preserve UMass seeks to balance development with the protection of the campus' most historic buildings and landscapes.

And there has been plenty to watch in recent years as the land of this plateau, on the edge of ancient Lake Hitchcock, has been dug up and concrete foundations poured like (almost) never before. A recreation center, a basketball arena, a new honors college complex, several new science buildings, new dorms, a new classroom building—all of these projects were completed in just fifteen years. Unlike previous growth eras, when the state and often the federal government

The W.E.B. Du Bois Library, Campus Pond, Lincoln Campus Center, and Lederle Graduate Research Center

footed the bill, this time it is the campus that is largely paying for it, out of its own operating budget. With little room in those budgets for hiring the biggest luminaries of the architecture world, quality construction and cautious design have characterized many of the more recent buildings. They fulfill important functions and do not offend. But few have lit up the architectural world or fired the imaginations. On the other hand, the urgent state of the environment has put growing emphasis on sustainability, with the campus constructing more energy-conscious buildings than their predecessors. The widely acclaimed perma-culture garden installed alongside Franklin Dining Hall in many ways brings the campus full circle, back to its origins in agricultural innovation and enterprise.

The debates about what UMass should be and what its buildings should say rage on. In each economic recession, the old debate about how important this campus is to the Commonwealth's future comes back, Lazarus-like. The pull of Massachusetts's long tradition of private schools, and past forty years of steadily growing skepticism toward government investment, is written as much in the cracks in buildings not well maintained as it is in new workaday campus buildings.

Standing on Mt. Sugarloaf a few miles north of the campus, where one can see the skyscrapers of UMass in the distance, the old academic village Olmsted and Manning had hoped for would never have been visible. Nor would Waugh's arboretum and the buildings and landscapes designed for an agricultural college. No, it is these monuments to a two-decade era when six million square feet were

Bartlett Hall, built in 1960, scheduled for demolition

added to the campus landscape that can be seen from afar. They document the progressive sensibility that has long characterized this campus.

But back at the university, standing in front of the Student Union, the past persists. It persists in the aluminum chairs scattered through halls and offices, green and orange remnants of the once-stylish and functional furniture that itself gestures backward to aircraft carriers, naval bases, and the world war that would bring thousands of new students to campus. It persists in unwieldy behemoths of desks and heavy filing cabinets, and in World War II–era linoleum floors and concrete block buildings. From the steps of the Student Union Building—to cite just a single example—one can see five styles of architecture, and buildings from three centuries. And in those styles, and the departments and research centers housed behind those facades, we can chart the growth of the public research university ideal over the past 150 years. That is the goal of the five tours in this book.

As we pass the sesquicentennial, we recognize that this book captures a snapshot in time. While there are centuries of built history (not to mention a millennium of Native American history) on the site, this is not a campus that has typically cherished tradition and heritage with regard to its built environment. Instead, this campus has pursued change and innovation. We are presently in the midst of another period of transformation, as a new campus plan moves toward implementation. Before long, the landscapes we describe here will again be altered. Someday, for example, the boulevard that is Massachusetts Avenue will be gone and new construction will enclose Haigis Mall. Soon buildings will rise on present-day parking lots. This is not to say that planners and designers had no respect for the past at UMass, nor that members of the university community are indifferent to the institution's physical heritage. But at UMass, the story is incomplete. It invites debate. And that is not such a bad thing for a university.

1   Alain de Botton, *The Architecture of Happiness* (New York: Pantheon, 2006), 157.

2   Harold Whiting Cary, *University of Massachusetts: A History of One Hundred Years* (Amherst: University of Massachusetts Press, 1962), 17.

3   "The 20 Ugliest Colleges in the USA," Campus Squeeze, http://www.campussqueeze.com/post/ The-20-Ugliest-Colleges-in-the-USA.aspx; on the Southwest Residential area being characterized as "brutal," see Katie Landeck, "Residential Life Continues to Roll Out Changes to Housing," *Daily Collegian,* January 31, 2012; Robert Campbell, "A Prototype, but Never to Be Repeated," *Boston Globe,* January 6, 1974.

4   Patricia Wright, "A Complex Edifice: Campus Skyscrapers Create Controversy," *Contact* 12 no. 2 (Winter 1987): 19; and http://www.archboston.org.

5   Arnold Friedmann, interview with Jessica Frankenfield, May 10, 2011.

6   de Botton, *Architecture of Happiness.* 168.

7   Marc Lécpold Benjamin Bloch, *The Historian's Craft*, trans. Peter Putnam (Manchester: Manchester University Press, 2004), 24.

8   *North Hedley Farmers Club Record Book,1856–63*, Special Collections and University Archives.

9   As quoted in *University of Massachusetts Amherst Historic Building Inventory: Final Survey Report,* 2009, 17.

10   Frederick Law Olmstead, "How Not to Establish an Agricultural College," *The Nation* 3, no. 69 (October 25, 1866): 335–36.

11   Ibid.

12   This discussion of Waugh relies heavily on Linda Flint McLelland's introduction to *Book of Landscape Gardening*, by Frank A. Waugh (Amherst: University of Massachusetts Press, 2006).

13   Jack Ahern, et al , Campus Physical Master Plan, 1993, 13.

14   As quoted in Ronald Story, ed., *Five Colleges: Five Histories* (Amherst: Five Colleges and Historic Deerfield, 1992), 62.

15   *Architectural Record* (May 1966), 165–84.

16   "Tradition will not Suffice," *The Alumnus* (February/March 1971), 3.

17   Deborah Klenotic. "Building Boom!" *Advancement Communications,* October 18, 2005.

Central Campus

1. Robsham Memorial Center for Visitors

2. Haigis Mall

3. Isenberg School of Management
   Harold Alfond Management Center

4. Whitmore Administration Building

5. Fine Arts Center

6. Herter Hall

7. Munson Hall

8. Curry Hicks

9. Bartlett Hall

10. Memorial Hall and Minuteman Crossing

11. Campus Pond

12. Old Chapel

13. Goodell Hall
    Helen Curtis Cole Commemorative Garden

14. South College

15. W. E. B. Du Bois Library

16. Machmer Hall
    Thompson Hall

17. Student Union

18. Murray D. Lincoln Campus Center and Parking Garage

19. Metawampe Lawn and Metawampe Sculpture

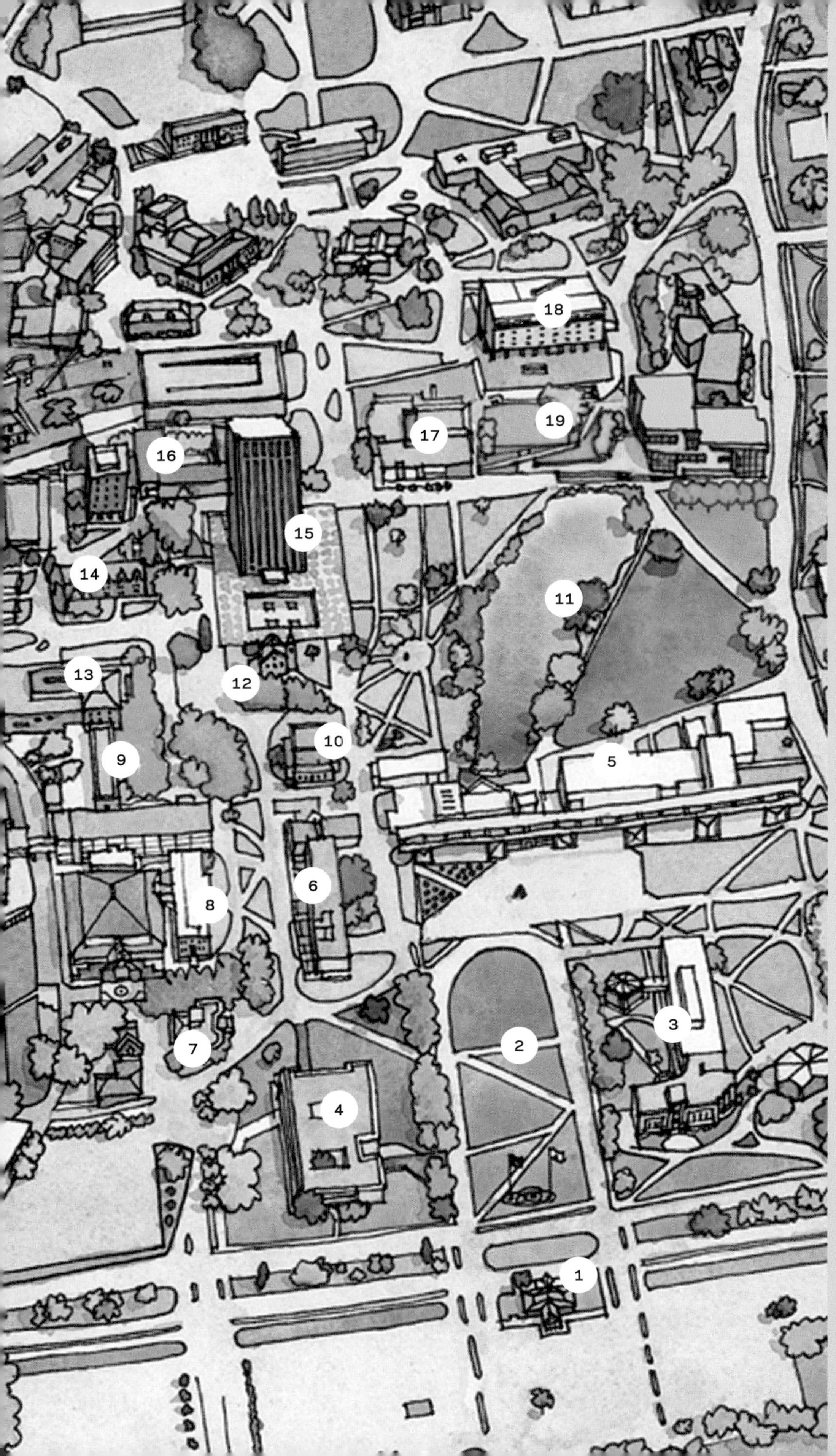
18
19
17
16
15
14
11
13
12
10
9
5
6
8
3
2
7
4
1

Walk One: Central Campus

From the vantage point of the contemporary Robsham Visitors Center, nothing seems to suggest the nineteenth-century agricultural school founded here in 1863, save perhaps for the grassy lawns. But even those lawns are in fact creations of a hundred years later, during the building boom of the 1960s.

The absence of Victorian structures from one's view is a sign of the truly remarkable and rapid transformation of the Massachusetts Agricultural College (MAC) into the Massachusetts State College (MSC, in 1931) and then again into the University of Massachusetts (in 1947). None of the buildings visible from the Robsham Center existed before 1964. If you stand today at the Center's Massachusetts Avenue entrance and look north, you can almost envision the now-lost landscapes. The Whitmore Administration Building stands atop farmland that, by World War I, had become MAC's athletic fields, and in particular the College's football field; the Isenberg School of Management and Haigis Mall itself fill in land once home to the campus's baseball diamond, and, in the foreground, the former soccer field. At the north end of Haigis Mall, at the top of the road called Presidents Drive, the Fine Arts Center occupies other one-time fields and a tree-lined road called Ellis Way.

As late as the 1960s, the campus still had an undeveloped quality and greenness to it that made it easy to see its roots as an agricultural college, but all of

Ellis Way to Memorial Hall in the 1920s

that changed with the post–World War II boom and the demand for (and demands of) a research university equal to the needs of the Commonwealth. The tumultuous decade that altered politics and culture across the United States also saw the dramatic transformation of UMass. Bold modernist buildings

In the early twentieth century, athletic fields occupied the space now claimed by Haigis Mall

rose on every corner of the campus, permanently altering the landscape's rural sensibility. But the connection to the past is not easily severed, and the built environment continued to look both backward and forward, inward and outward as the community worked to forge a new identity as an institution engaged in research and innovation. When created in summer 1968, for instance, Haigis Mall was lined with seventy littleleaf linden trees in two double rows, a treatment also found on the iconic New England town commons and one comparable to the double rows of trees (Lombardy poplars, and later elms) that since the early nineteenth century have ornamented the spectacular seventeenth-century common that still survives in neighboring Hadley. Massachusetts Avenue, a four-lane boulevard lined with 175 London plane trees marking the southern edge of campus, alludes to the width of Boston's 1880s Commonwealth Avenue. As new circulation patterns and the need to balance the demands of pedestrian and vehicular traffic became imperative following the dramatic postwar expansion of automobility, these spaces invoked both continuity and change.

The shift, from an agricultural campus to an urban campus in a rural setting, had been settled with the 1962 Campus Plan by Sasaki, Walker and Associates of Boston. While much of the plan was ignored, as has often been the case with UMass master plans, the campus was fundamentally changed by its recommendations. Central to Sasaki's vision was to reorient the campus along a long avenue on the western ridge of "Mass Aggie's" site, and make way for a series of modern buildings.

The buildings in the central campus are, for the most part, emblems of the university era, which began in 1947, nearly a century after the MAC was founded. Under the leadership of a series of presidents whose names have made their way on to important buildings (Ralph Van Meter, John Paul Mather, John W. Lederle), the MSC became a major university, with a unified College of Arts and Sciences, a graduate school, and a series of professional schools. By the end of the university's growth spurt, in the 1970s, the university ballooned from 4,000 students in 1954 to 20,000 just twenty years later. The establishment of the university—a watershed development long proposed and long delayed—demanded a fresh approach to the built environment, and these leaders found it in the powerful imagery of modern architecture.

Hicks Way, which travels from the north end of the Whitmore Administration Building to the W. E. B. Du Bois Library, remains the central pedestrian pathway of the campus. Named for longtime athletic director Curry Hicks, who died in 1963, Hicks Way was once an extension of Amherst's Lincoln Avenue—one of the several town streets named after Civil War leaders, including General George B. McClellan. The imprint of the avenue is a useful reminder to the campus community that it was President Abraham Lincoln who signed the Morrill Land Grant Act, which created many of America's finest public universities, in 1862, in the midst of rebellion.

1. Robsham Memorial Center for Visitors
Eric Jahan of KJA Architects, 1998

Unlike many campuses, the University of Massachusetts has no main gate, no pre-ferred approach. Visitors traveling to UMass from points north, south, and west often arrive via Interstate 91 and then routes 9 or 116, finally approaching campus along North Hadley Road, a pathway that leads toward this neighboring village-within-a-small-town that was so integral to the campus's creation. Today North Hadley Road becomes Massachusetts Avenue, leading travelers up a rise from the lowlands toward the plateau on which the main campus stands; their first glimpse of the campus takes in the profiles of the high-rises that are the Kennedy and Coolidge residence halls before their gaze inevitably sweeps north across the playing fields and recreational facilities. Traffic from the town of Amherst to the south arrives at this same spot via North Pleasant Street, which bends westward into Massachusetts Avenue. In order to offer visitors a greater sense of arrival, in recent years a series of signs marking the campus's various entries have appeared, but the effect is nevertheless more gradual than marked.

Campus planners in the 1960s sought to remedy that gap by creating a more impressive landscape that would serve as the main entrance to the University, at the intersection of a wide boulevard and a grassy mall. At the foot of that mall today stands the Robsham Visitors Center. Named in memory of E. Paul Robsham Jr. (a deceased son of a UMass trustee), this visitors center is an understated start to a tour of the campus. When it was constructed directly opposite the monumental Fine Arts Center, flanked by the Whitmore Administration Building and the Isenberg School of Management, the red brick structure with its steep, angular hipped roof and arched lunettes—intended to conjure impressions of a New England carriage house—completed the rectangle of buildings around Haigis Mall. Architect Eric Jahan chose a domestic-scale vocabulary. With conscious nods to the iconic New England shingle style, and described with a wink by Jahan as a "Picturesque Regional" style, this comfortable adaptation of historical styles (common in the postmodern era of the late twentieth century) plays its role well and offers a humble yet welcoming entry to the University campus.[1]

2. Haigis Mall
Sasaki Associates, 1962

The Campus Pond and its environs are often considered the University's living room, which suggests then that Haigis Mall is the foyer, providing an inviting expanse of lawn to greet arrivals to campus. This landscape was created in 1968, on the site of Alumni Field. An early twentieth-century sketch shows the field about 1914, when student volunteers helped prepare the land for an array of recreational and athletic uses. The design at this time included a football field encircled by a track as well as a baseball diamond and tennis courts, though these were not altogether realized—tennis appar-ently lacked sufficient local appeal—and by 1947 soccer fields occupied that space.

When envisioned in the 1960s, Haigis Mall was part of a larger plan to encircle the campus with a peripheral road system that would separate the academic core from the residential areas. While the belief (articulated in the 1966 yearbook) that "once the road is completed, there will be no cars on the academic campus" was never realized, the new landscape also created this grand mall in place of the old playing fields. By 1968 the new roads and mall were under construction; a large parking area stretched between the forthcoming Massachusetts Avenue and the Lincoln Apartments (Louis Warren Ross, 1949), swallowing what was once the western end of Phillips Avenue. A U-shaped path was designed to arc from Massachusetts Avenue, along the School of Business Administration (today the Isenberg School of Management), and across the facade of the Fine Arts Center before reversing course and returning to the four-lane, tree-lined boulevard.

The Mall was named for John William Haigis Sr., a local newspaperman who also served in the Massachusetts legislature and in 1929 rose to become lieutenant governor; he was also among the University's trustees. He established the radio station WHAI and was the founding editor of the *Greenfield Recorder*.

Today Haigis Mall serves as the first and last landscape many travelers to campus encounter. Local and regional transit buses arrive and depart from the Mall, and the hundreds of schoolchildren who visit UMass on class field trips every year disembark here as well. At the start of the academic year, the marching band—particularly the drum and flag corps—uses the broad lawn to rehearse. Pow-wows occasionally hosted by the campus have unfolded on this space, as have events aimed to entertain the student body: in 2011 UMass Dining Services built a 12-foot frying pan on Haigis Mall, setting a new world record for the world's largest stir fry.

From top left to bottom right: McGuirk Alumni Stadium, Southwest Residential Area, Massachusetts Avenue, Whitmore Administration Building, Haigis Mall, and the School of Business Administration

The 1964 Business Administration building

3. Isenberg School of Management
Axel Kaufmann of Campbell and Aldrich, 1964

Harold Alfond Management Center
Architecture Resources Cambridge (ARC), 2002

For those who had been lobbying since around 1910 for the agricultural college to become a comprehensive university, one of the driving forces was the need for a course of study in business management. Individual courses in the field were offered in the 1930s and 1940s, but only with the expectation that the College would become a university in 1947 did planning for a full-fledged business school begin. Growing out of the Department of Economics, the business program accepted students in the fall of 1946; a school of business was created in 1950 and accredited in 1958. It was, at that time, one of just four New England schools of business administration to receive national accreditation. Students flocked to the new school, then located in Draper Hall: by 1954 there were 550 undergraduates enrolled in the school, more than in the College of Agriculture.

A dedicated building to house the School of Management opened in 1964. It was designed by Axel Kaufmann of Campbell and Aldrich, the firm that would soon provide the design for the Whitmore Administration Building across the way and the Lederle Graduate Research Center on the north end of campus. The building's main block—intended from the outset to accommodate teaching as well as applied and basic research—is a three-story, thirty-classroom building, with a top floor for faculty

Two freestanding hexagonal auditoriums flank the business school.

The Harold Alfond Management Center

offices (demarcated by a series of narrow windows). The building's four bays are asymmetric. The north bay, clad in brick, is largely blank, interrupted only by a series of tall, thin windows. A narrow entrance bay, projecting slightly beyond the facade, is flanked by two broad sections lit with large windows, while the band of vertical fenestration across the top unifies the design. Upon completion, the University congratulated itself on the opening of a business administration building with "crisp, sleek lines" and excellent acoustics in its two auditoriums.[2]

These two adjoining eight-sided auditoriums, accessed by freestanding hexagonal structures, seat 254 and 485. The hexagonal shape was an intriguing break from typical lecture halls. The idea—largely borne out—is that the design accommodates many students without requiring anyone to sit a long way from the instructor. Though Mahar Auditorium holds nearly 500 people, no one sits further than fifteen rows away from the lecturer. The larger of the two auditoriums, Mahar was named after Senator Ralph C. Mahar of Orange, who was central to several pieces of legislation that helped the young university gain greater control over curriculum, hiring, and construction—all essential to the University becoming competitive on the national stage.

In 2002 Architecture Resources Cambridge (ARC) completed an addition to the southern end of the School of Management building. The Harold Alfond Management Center provided technologically advanced classrooms for the growing business school, as well as a three-story glass atrium for a school that had no common gathering place. The nearly 50,000-square-foot addition, oriented perpendicular to the earlier structure, helped to create something of a courtyard for the school and provide an entrance on Massachusetts Avenue. The wide Jerusalem-stone facing is a sharp contrast to the subdued brick and concrete of the original building.

The Center is named after Harold and Dorothy Alfond, founders of Dexter Shoe Corporation and donors to a number of New England colleges. The School of Management itself was renamed for alumnus and donor Eugene Isenberg, chairman and CEO of Nabors Industries. The Alfond Center was significant for the Isenberg School, of course. But it also marked the start of a major new era of building on the campus, one that continued through the first two decades of the new century.

The west elevation of the Whitmore Administration Building, looking north toward the W. E. B. Du Bois Library

4. Whitmore Administration Building
Campbell & Aldrich, 1967

At first glance the Whitmore Administration Building looks as if it were designed, fortresslike, to withstand assault; the earthen berm, deep windows, and concrete sunshades seem inspired by the narrow firing stations of medieval castles. But the building was completed in 1967, before some of the most contentious protests of the late 1960s and 1970s; while urban legend at UMass attributes its defensive appearance to student unrest, in 1967 those days were still to come.

By the time drawings for a new administration building were on the boards, a vision had emerged that would situate the new structure in a very different context from the Business Administration School it would face. The business school, when constructed, fronted on fields still devoted to recreation and sport; Sasaki's 1962 plan meant that it would stand alongside the new grassy mall, a factor that helped up the ante in terms of the need for a significant architectural statement. In fact, Whitmore was originally sited within the expanse that is now the lawn: the building was moved westward when planners realized that it would disrupt the effect of the mall leading to the campus's chief portico—the Fine Arts Center.

Campbell & Aldrich, the Boston-based firm specializing in college and institutional buildings, was designing the low-lying Whitmore at the same moment it was envisioning UMass's first skyscraper, the Lederle Graduate Research Building. The two structures together brought modernism to campus, but in two very different forms.

This leafy atrium outside a small cafeteria provides respite for students, faculty, and staff.

Despite the bunkerish feel today attributed to the administration building, the large, open courtyard at the building's center is more representative of the architects' vision when the building was drafted. This airy enclave makes for a pleasing gathering space and brings light deep into what otherwise appears to be a solid mass of concrete; in the courtyard garden, Carolina hemlock, black tupelo, star magnolia, rhododendron, and Japanese pieris create an environment both cheerful and serene. A second light well, though not accessible to foot traffic, offers natural light to additional offices, ensuring that workers inside remain connected with the outdoors.

The earliest exposed concrete structure to be erected on campus (plans had already begun to take shape for the Fine Arts Center, but Whitmore was completed first), the low, wide building—its ground floor concealed behind sloping grass—seems to sink into the land; yet the rhythm of the recessed windows provides relief from the weight of the concrete, lightening the overall effect, while the terracing of the upper floors also softens the design. On the northern end, the almost whimsical 200-foot ramp (long used by students and town children to pick up speed on bikes and skateboards) also loosens the starkness of the building and conveys the sense of crossing over a moat. Long before the Americans with Disabilities Act transformed landscapes nationwide, the campus built its share of ramps that eased access and enlivened its buildings.

The building was named after Phillip Whitmore, who served the University in many capacities—as president of the Alumni Association, trustee, and state representative. It remains home to the offices of the chancellor, provost, and most of the upper administrative staff, and so has indeed come to serve as the target for many of the student protests that have unfolded on campus. Stormed, occupied, and chanted at, the Whitmore Administration Building remains a focal point for the campus community.

5. Fine Arts Center
Roche, Dinkeloo and Associates, 1974; lobby addition, Perry Dean Rogers, 1997; Quinnipiac, Robert Murray, 1975 (refurbished & reinstalled 2004)

The Fine Arts Center is perhaps the most important work of modern architecture on campus and the most controversial. It was highly praised and criticized in its day, and remains a touchstone in the debate about UMass architecture. That is understandable and in line with the ambition of Kevin Roche, the architect. Robert Campbell, architecture critic of the *Boston Globe*, said correctly when the building opened that "of all today's architects, the one who always seems to come up with the biggest, boldest, most original ideas is Kevin Roche." Born in Dublin, Ireland, Roche studied at the font

Upon construction, two broad reflecting pools gestured toward the Campus Pond.

of modernism, Mies van der Rohe's Illinois Institute of Technology. He joined the firm of Eero Saarinen in 1950 and by 1953 became its chief designer. The firm later changed its name to Roche and Dinkeloo and designed some of the most innovative buildings of the 1960s and 1970s, including the Dulles International Airport (1962), the Vivian Beaumont Theater at Lincoln Center (1965)—for which he completed the work of Eero Saarinen—the Rochester Institute of Technology (1969), the Oakland Museum of Art (1996), and, perhaps most famously, the Ford Foundation Headquarters in New York (1968). Roche was awarded architecture's highest honor, the Pritzker Prize, in 1982, and the American Institute of Architects Gold Medal in 1993.

At the time of its design, in 1968, the Fine Arts Center was an innovation on American campuses. Before this time, no campus, public or private, had a facility of this scope and ambition. UMass commissioned designs for a huge complex of interconnected arts facilities comprising 220,000 gross square feet, four auditoriums (including one exceeding 2,000 seats), the University Gallery, 17 classrooms, 75 studios, and 56 faculty offices. At a cost of $13.8 million, it was also one of the most expensive buildings on the campus. No other New England school had such an extensive arts complex; the Fine Arts Center made Amherst a stopping point for major music, theater, and dance productions. Roche would continue this approach with Wesleyan's arts center, and other colleges soon followed suit.

This massive building, stretching the length of two football fields and then some, is in a way fairly simple in organization. A series of volumes are held together by an elevated 646-foot-long "bridge" of north-facing studios. The dramatically angled roofline on the east elevation coupled with the extraordinarily long facade have given rise to an urban legend that the building was designed to allude to a (very) grand piano, but the architect has rejected this notion. Instead, the combination of shapes responds to other aims. The most dramatic move by Roche—who aimed to provide a "grand entrance to the whole campus," since one "really didn't exist"—was to create an inverse gateway: instead of a marking the entrance to the building and campus with architectural elements, he instead left a massive void at the building's center so that the eye was drawn through the building, toward the Campus Pond, and into the physical and symbolic heart of the campus. The gravitational pull was accentuated by two angled reflecting pools, which once lay beneath the "bridge" and by the wide staircase leading from the gateway down to the Pond. From the openness of Haigis Mall, visitors were to be brought into the covered gateway and then urged outward, down to the Pond. The *Globe* critic, Campbell, said simply that "urbanistically, it's a brilliant concept." [3] And this is precisely what Roche was after—an urbanistic building for a university that was becoming a small city after having spent a century as a small village. The 1974 yearbook (the *Index*) applauded this building, "the newest member in our long line of architectural wonders." [4]

Among the stunning interior spaces are a 2,000-seat concert hall and a smaller recital hall. As the University's ambition expanded in the 1960s, the limited quality of existing performance and rehearsal spaces had inhibited the administration's ability to bring high-caliber artists to campus. A performance by the Chicago Symphony in the Cage ("bordering on the comic," according to one observer) threw into bold relief the need for a better venue, and even though it was fairly new, the beautiful 1957 Student Union Ballroom had not been designed with performers in mind.[5] Bowker Auditorium was the only option, and it wasn't prepared to accommodate theater. As a result, plans for the FAC included a concert hall. In order to incorporate as many seats as possible, Roche aimed to make it "very sort of tight, and keep it as close" as possible, to "make the connection between the audience and the stage as tight as we could make it, so that you didn't have the feeling of being in an enormous room." [6]

The balconies in the FAC concert hall move forward, toward the stage, rather than retreating to the hall's heights.

To create the desired number of seats, the space is wide. Most notably, while it is more common to see balconies recede further and further from the stage, here stacks of mezzanines reach forward rather than stretching back, moving closer and closer as they extend higher and higher. Put another way, the cheap seats get you closer to the action.

Meanwhile, other observers noted the initial omission of a recital hall, something of a smaller scale that would be suitable for more intimate performances. "Of the many Fine Arts or Music buildings in the last fifteen years in this country," Philip Bezanson, chairman of the Music Department from 1964 to 1973, would inform administrators, "all, to my knowledge, have recital halls."[7] A space originally planned to house a faculty lounge was subsequently redesigned to hold a small auditorium. Because the decision was made late in the planning process, the walls were not soundproofed, and other problems marred the experience for performers and audience alike.

The University Museum of Contemporary Art is nestled underneath the main auditorium, with an entrance facing the Pond. Not surprisingly, the museum has long suffered from lack of visibility. Until 2011 called the University Gallery, it is the largest of the six galleries on campus (the others being the Augusta Savage and Wheeler galleries in the Central Residential Area, the Hampden Gallery in Southwest, the Herter Art Gallery, and the Student Union Gallery). Today plans are afoot to find a bigger and more visible home for this collection of over 2,600 works on paper, a teaching facility and a "forum where renowned and emerging artists can test ideas and where diverse audiences can participate in cultural experiences that enhance understanding of the art of our time."[8]

The FAC has had its share of critics. For many, the building is a massive concrete intruder, a rough-edged monster. In fact, this modernist structure was one of the most thoughtful about its surroundings of any buildings of that era. While it represented a radical change to the Campus Pond landscape, the building is deeply respectful of Olmsted's vision of the Campus Pond as the emotional heart of the campus. The front of the Fine Arts Center draws people to the Pond; the pond-facing side creates a border that accentuates the pond landscape as an outdoor "room." Indeed, Roche imagined concerts performed on the pond's south end, with the audience sitting on steps leading up to the auditorium and theater entrances.

Furthermore, while the new plans and buildings of the 1960s and 1970s eliminated the tree-lined boulevard called Ellis Way—which ran from North Pleasant Street up to what is now Hicks Way, and all the way around what is now the Campus Center— Roche offered a substitute: a 30-foot-high covered passageway running the length

The formerly open passageway between Haigis Mall and the Campus Pond was enclosed in 1997 to create a lobby for the Fine Arts Center concert hall

of the massive building, from North Pleasant (and all the residential dormitories on Orchard Hill) to Herter Hall. It remains one of the grandest walkways on campus and one of the busiest.

Drawing students to the walkway was integral to Roche's vision: the architect had as a goal making the arts integral to the University. He wanted students to pass continually by the concert hall, theater, and University Gallery, and under the studios in the course of their daily lives.

At the inauguration of the building in 1975, the crowd of legislators and administrators were joined by the poet, writer, and Librarian of Congress Archibald MacLeish. "What I hear about your Center for the Arts—the building and the concept—encourages me," he said. He continued:

> You propose to steer clear of the whirlpool and the rock and head for the unmarked channel in between—vocationalism to starboard, museumism to port, and a fair passage on ahead to the great discovery. Meaning by great discovery, of course, the landfall of the meeting of art and man: the meeting of the work of art as a work of art and the observer not as observer but as living, breathing human being. In that encounter the work of art is not, as in a museum, an end product but a continuing process, and the student is exercising not his critical faculties alone but his human creativity, his essential self.... I am glad it was made in this Republic where the Revolution of Man was first declared.[9]

Over the years, the building has evolved in ways that have been no less controversial than the original construction. One problem was recognized even before the building opened. The Fine Arts Center was billed as a classroom and lab building with theaters and an auditorium so that it would not be seen as directly competing with Springfield's Symphony Hall. To make this ruse defensible, the auditorium (the Concert Hall) had no box office, coat room, loading dock, or green room—all essential elements of a performing arts center. Similarly, there was no formal lobby for patrons: in chilly New England, the hall opened directly on the concrete plaza. The signature gesture of the gateway void became problematic, as it created a wind tunnel while denying the audience a place to gather before performances in the theater and large auditorium, or in which to mingle during intermissions. Perry Dean Rogers Architects of Boston was tapped in 1994 to address these problems. They designed the channel glass and lead-coated copper lobby that serves the Rand Theater and the Concert Hall. The lobby is composed of three cubes. The cube to the north is the lighthouse, which reflects an inviting yellow glow on the Pond at night. To the south, the lobby presents a marquee that on show nights is lit to cycle through the color spectrum. The lobby was awarded the BSA Honor Award for Excellence in 2000, but its insertion also destroyed one of the central gestures of Roche's building.

The need to alter Roche's design to create a lobby for the Fine Arts Center has been matched by the need to address other problems with the building. In 2002 the Bezanson Recital Hall was given a long-overdue overhaul by Peter Turowski for Margo Jones Architects. New lobby space was created by enclosing the walkway between

the original hall and the offices of the Department of Music and Dance. In order to make a softer space more appealing to current aesthetics, the refurbished hall was enhanced by maple detailing set off by matte stainless steel; the stage is maple as well. New soundproofing and lighting complete the effect.

The lack of maintenance that affected many buildings of the 1960s and 1970s hit the innovative Fine Arts Center particularly hard—a number of sections of that 646-foot bridge leak, for example. The building was also compromised by the University's decision to add more faculty and students to a building designed for fewer numbers. And many have, perhaps justifiably, complained of the difficulty of moving from one part of the building to another, undermining the effort to combine the arts that was one of the original goals of the project.

The FAC plaza has also evolved from its initial appearance. Two triangular reflecting pools were integral to Roche's original design, connecting the building with the Campus Pond visible through the void, giving the massive structure a sense that it was floating on water, and directing visitors toward the covered passageway and into the heart of the campus. Leaky and then neglected, in time the pools were drained. In 2001 the eastern pool was removed and replaced with a thirty-two-space parking area, just one of the many offerings to the ever-hungry parking deity. (Across campus, attractive grassy areas, such as in front of Fernald or in the Northeast Quad, have also been given over to parking. The latest campus plan promises, as have previous plans, to conquer the beast and return pedestrians to their rightful place at the top of the food chain.)

In 2004 the western pool was likewise replaced, this time with a garden landscape (funded in part by the Class of 1954 and designed by William Cannon, an Easthampton landscape architect and 1973 graduate; Chris Riddle of the Amherst firm Kuhn Riddle served as the architect for the project). A concrete bridge creates a strong diagonal across the plaza and spans a pebbled area containing large boulders of Worthington stone amid ornamental grasses. Louvered steel benches sit alongside a planting of

Robert Murray's Quinnipiac *(1975)*

ferns intended to cue a stream bank, while honey locusts will in time provide a verdant archway for pedestrians.

As much as it has changed through the years, the plaza remains, however, a stage for *Quinnipiac,* a work of abstract art that was part of the Fine Arts Center Gallery's initial exhibit, Artist and Fabricator, in 1975. Canadian-American artist Robert Murray's sheet-metal sculpture was—like the building it complements—controversial from the moment of its installation. Like Murray's other work, this 18-foot high, 15,000-pound outdoor work was made by cutting, bending, and twisting steel plate. It reflects a moment

The 646-foot-long "art bridge" creates the grandest pedestrian avenue on the campus.

when Murray's work began taking freer forms; here, crunches and folded edges create an archlike opening, with negative space beneath. Murray titled the work *Quinnipiac* not because the bent steel sheets were meant to symbolize the river but simply because his studio lay right alongside the waterway. Rather than a literal gesture, the work—now the jewel in the crown of Haigis Mall—is better understood as a "dialogue between two sheets of steel," as an FAC Gallery exhibit catalog proposes. "Its design, full of curves, straight edges, and diagonal edges, with its undulating surface, creates a changing play of light and shadow. The curves of the sculpture in front of the sharp defined lines of the FAC, make it stand out even more." [10]

6. Herter Hall
Coletti Brothers, 1969

At crucial juncture between the drama of the Fine Arts Center, the cool reserve of Whitmore, and the welcoming Victorian brick Munson Hall, Herter Hall is the Brutalist anchor to the start of Hicks Way, the central spine of the campus.

Students and faculty rolling down Whitmore's ramp next pass this 1969 structure designed by the Coletti Brothers of Boston. The Colettis were architect and watercolorist Carroll Coletti, who trained at the Boston Architectural Center and the Yale School of Architecture, and his brother Paul. Today the Coletti firm is best known for its restrained modernism, including the Salisbury boathouse and pavilion, chosen by the U.S. State Department for exhibition at the Brussels World's Fair; a series of high schools; the Quincy City Hospital Annex; and a sympathetic addition to H. H. Richardson's renowned Crane Memorial Library in Quincy.

Accustomed to designing brick-facaded institutional buildings, the firm broke new ground with their dual Brutalist pieces, Herter and Tobin halls (1972). The term *Brutalist* seems off-putting from the start—conjuring as it does notions of savagery or cruelty, something crushingly inhumane. The negative resonances of the English translation of a French phrase—*béton brut,* or "raw concrete"—have been hard to shake for buildings of this period. In its original formulation, though, the term invoked an exploration of any material's fundamental properties. In the words of two of the movement's founders, Alison and Peter Smithson, "Brutalism tries to face up to a mass-production society, and drag a rough poetry out of the confused and powerful forces which are at work." [11] This sensibility, then—the search for the "rough poetry" of materials in their raw state—infuses not only Herter Hall but its companions across campus.

Herter Hall is a workhorse of a building, housing many of the humanities departments that could no longer squeeze into the Chapel or Bartlett

Upon completion, Herter Hall and its annex stretched alongside the top of Haigis Mall.

The dynamic west elevation of Herter Hall

Hall when the University started its massive expansion in the 1960s. (There remains a tunnel under Hicks Way, connecting these core buildings of a past College of Arts and Sciences.) The main block of the building is a seven-story slab; its structure (staircase and elevator shafts) and materials (large sections of precast concrete) are not hidden but instead are left exposed to announce the building's engineering. While some observers today find the mass of gray concrete off-putting, the architects intended the design to cultivate a sense of approachability. For instance, the building's interior functions are reflected through its facade, leaving no mystery about where visitors should travel. The first two floors, containing classroom space, are differentiated by massing and fenestration. On the comparatively austere eastern and front elevation, the classrooms retreat slightly from the upper five floors (which contain academic offices), while a series of balconies draw attention to interior gathering places. The west facade, facing Hicks Way, is perhaps more interesting, with two levels of classrooms pushing right up to the roadway, allowing for stacks of fifty-seat classrooms to fit into a relatively narrow building site. The asymmetrical interior layout of the building breaks with traditional form: the position of the elevator shafts and opposing balconies asserts that the core of each floor is offset, positioned toward the building's southern half.

On the interior, the office floors are also asymmetric, with rooms along the building's east elevation comparatively smaller than those along the west (suggesting that the Colettis had perhaps little experience with academic personalities). On the north end are well-appointed lounges in which wooden bands over metal mesh warm otherwise plain interiors. On the opposite ends of these halls are small seminar rooms. The fact that the building is long on classrooms and short on seminar rooms may reflect the relative weight of graduate training in the humanities in the mid-1960s.

Herter Annex, connected to Herter Hall via a glass walkway, contains gallery space and two large lecture halls, their slope indicated by low-relief channels on the exterior.

Herter Annex, connected to the main block by a glass walkway at the second story, holds an art gallery below and two large lecture halls above. Here, too, the building is intended to be legible from the exterior; the slope of the auditorium within is marked in low relief on the concrete walls, while ground-floor office spaces and a seminar room are visible behind plates of glass.

The building is named after Massachusetts Governor and U.S. Secretary of State Christian Herter. Herter's political accomplishments aside, the honor may have been given as much because of Herter's championing of a bill (known at the time as the "Freedom Bill") that gave the University the right to hire and pay faculty and staff according to its own criteria. This was crucial in making the University a nationally competitive research university.

7. Munson Hall
Emory A. Ellsworth, 1898

Standing between two monuments of the postwar era, this inviting brick building—an eclectic mix of the Queen Anne, Georgian, and Richardson Romanesque languages—appears to fit better with residential Lincoln Avenue, of which Hicks Way is the extension. Designed at the close of the nineteenth century by Emory A. Ellsworth, architect of other campus buildings of the era (East and West Experiment Station), the building initially housed the campus's first large animal veterinary laboratory. Until the 1980s, the original crane rail used for conveying carcasses to the upstairs laboratory was still in place in the basement. The building was originally named for James B. Paige, the veterinary professor who oversaw the building's construction. Later, a new Paige laboratory building was built on the north end of campus, and this building was renamed Munson Hall, after Willard Munson, a football star from

Munson Hall

1904 who returned to campus to become the director of the Extension Service, which was housed in the building.

Munson Hall is home today to the University's communications and public relations offices. One of the more notable moments in the building's history involves the visit of Amy Carter, the daughter of President Jimmy Carter, who came to campus in 1987 to protest CIA recruiting; she and 1960s activist Abbie Hoffman led a group (having failed to penetrate the more formidable Whitmore Administration building) to occupy Munson Hall for six hours to bring attention to the covert involvement of the CIA in Central America.

The Annex just behind the building once sheltered sick horses; in recent years it held sculpture studios for the Art Department after it had grown beyond the confines of the Fine Arts Center. In 2012 plans emerged to demolish the Annex.

8. Curry Hicks
Clinton F. Goodwin, 1931

Designed by MAC alumnus Clinton Goodwin (who refused to accept fees for his efforts), Curry Hicks, named after a longtime director of athletics and student health, was a dramatic improvement over athletic facilities of the college. The long building fronting on Hicks Way is one of the most classically inspired of UMass buildings, with its strong central pediment echoed in a later addition. But Goodwin gestured to local tradition by including the broken-pediment doorway common to Colonial-era homes of the Connecticut Valley. This element appears on a number of UMass buildings, including Skinner Hall (1948).

For a fuller discussion of this building, see Walk Four.

This view of the east elevation of Curry Hicks shows the Georgian resonance of the original building.

Bartlett Hall's west elevation

9. Bartlett Hall
Shepley, Bulfinch, Richardson & Abbott, 1960

Bartlett Hall, home to the College of Arts and Sciences that had been created in 1955 (and named for attorney Joseph W. Bartlett, a trustee of the University from 1934 to 1960), captures the architectural tension of the UMass campus—between traditional New England architecture and avant-garde modernism—as few other buildings do. The successor to H. H. Richardson, architect of Boston's Trinity Church, Shepley, Bulfinch, Richardson & Abbott's best-known campus work had been for Stanford University, begun in 1888.

Built on the site of the Drill Hall (1883, what the alumni magazine at the time called "that old soldier among university structures," military training facilities having been required as part of the Morrill Act, passed a year into the Civil War), Bartlett has two wings arranged in an L shape, each gesturing stylistically in different directions. The main building, parallel to Hicks Way, is a fairly typical and elegant example of institutional architecture of the late 1950s (not unlike the high schools that the Coletti Brothers had designed before their concrete buildings on the UMass campus). The rigorously modernist building was clad with a brick facade in order to speak to surrounding buildings, such as Curry Hicks and Munson Hall. This wing's best face is actually the side looking west, where a broad plaza gives the building a grander status than its more humble fronting onto Hicks Way.

Conversely, a second wing, connected to the more formal block by three stacked glass corridors and sited perpendicularly to Hicks Way, offers the nearest example of early modernism adapted from Europe in the 1920s and after. The wing appears as a light counterpoint to the north wing, with a wooden facade of windows divided into ever smaller sections, in a busy constellation of windows and panels painted blue. There is the faintest echo of the original Bauhaus building in Dessau, Germany.

This building houses the English Department as well as Women's Studies, Art History, and Journalism. Plagued by structural problems, it is now slated for demolition.

10. Memorial Hall and Minuteman Crossing

James H. Ritchie, 1920; figure by John Townsend, 2007;
stonework by John Sendelbach

The contrasts of design continue along the campus's central spine. Nestled across from the Bauhaus-inspired Bartlett Hall, in the shadow of the Gothic Chapel, in line with the Brutalist Herter, is the University's lone Italian Renaissance–inspired building, the rigorous brick and sandstone Memorial Hall. The stylistic choice was no accident. Architect James H. Ritchie (1876–1964) wrote that his goal was to make a "monumental design which will differentiate it from the buildings that are devoted to instruction." [12]

Scottish-born Ritchie would become a significant figure in shaping the UMass campus, as he and landscape architect Warren H. Manning collaborated over the course of both men's careers. Ritchie came to the United States as the four-year-old son of a Scottish shoemaker; by 1900 he was working as a draughtsman alongside his younger brother George, an apprentice architect. He and Manning both contributed designs to Virginia's Jamestown tercentenary, and it is likely that that collaboration figured in Ritchie's coming to have a significant effect on UMass.

Manning (1860–1938) and Ritchie (1876–1964) collaborated on a number of projects throughout their careers, with Ritchie designing the building and Manning planning the grounds. The two men perhaps met when Manning served as landscape designer for the 1907 Jamestown Exposition; Ritchie was among the team of architects who helped design various buildings for the grounds. They must have hit it off: as early as 1908, the two responded to an invitation to submit plans for a redesigned campus at the University of Minnesota. When Manning was hired to plan a model town for William Gwinn Mather's Cleveland-Cliffs Iron Company near its Gwinn, Michigan, mine, Ritchie contributed plans for the train station. The pair would also join forces on an 1918 housing project in Lowell, Massachusetts, and the 1932 hotel that Mather (among Manning's longtime clients) built in Ishpeming, Michigan.

Ritchie would go on to enjoy a long series of commissions in Amherst. Next to Louis Warren Ross, he would be the most prolific of UMass architects. In addition to the campus buildings described here, his works in Amherst include the Ray Stannard Baker House at 118 Sunset Avenue (which later served as the Sigma Alpha Epsilon Fraternity house) and the Lincoln Building at 40-50 Main Street. Ritchie's work in Boston includes the Boston Consumptives Hospital.

Memorial Hall, built in 1921 entirely with donations, is the University's testament to students who have fallen in war. It was built immediately after World War I to honor the fifty-one MAC men who died in what was assumed to be the "war to end all wars." Over time Memorial Hall became the de facto tribute to all fallen alumni. In addition to the numerous engagements of the Great War, lintels of the building now bear the names of battles from later wars—World War II, Korea, Vietnam, Iraq. But despite the impact of the war, it was hard to raise enough money to pay for the building as designed. In order to economize, many of the architectural elements that would otherwise have

been made of granite were actually executed in wood, including the decorative corbels around the windows on the first floor on the Pond side. The building also features memorial plaques and trees on the Campus Pond side.

The alumni who led the movement to create Memorial Hall had an intriguing notion of how to remember their fallen comrades. While the building had—and still has—a room dedicated to the memory of those who died in war, central to the idea was that this structure would be a living, active student center. The memorial was, according to a 1920 article, "consecrated as a student activities center," with rooms for rehearsals, a college store, billiards, even a basement bowling alley.[13] The motto engraved in Memorial Hall—"we will keep faith with you who lie asleep"—was understood to mean that the Hall should be a place of bustling activity, not merely solemnity.

In 1946 alumni worked hard to dramatically expand the building to honor those who had fallen in World War II. Plans were made by the architect Clinton Goodwin, one of the designers of Goodell Library, to add a large wing. Advocates never raised enough money and ultimately the idea was dropped. But the Student Union, built in 1957, answered the need for a gathering place for students and their organizations. Memorial Hall, once owned by the Alumni Association, still holds the association's offices.

An impulse to honor veterans also informed the installation of *The Minuteman*, a bronze figure funded by the Class of 1950 (the same class that commissioned the Chief Metawampe statue just east of the Student Union as its graduation gift). In many ways, the artwork is an artifact of the powerful impact of World War II on the campus. "Our class was the veterans class," Donald R. Progulske observed at the work's dedication: "There were about 1,100 men and women in the class, and at least 900 of them were veterans." When contemplating a gift as the class approached its fiftieth anniversary, the alumni "chose the Minuteman because it is a patriotic symbol."[14] Cast and poured at the Paul King Foundry in Rhode Island, the "life-and-a-half" scale sculpture of the minuteman, as envisioned by retired UMass art professor John Townsend, depicts the farmer-turned-soldier striding off to battle. The 9-foot-tall, 1,200-pound figure, which stands on a gray granite base, is caught midstride, a rifle slung over his right shoulder, his barrel to the ground to protect its powder, heading eastward to Lexington and Concord.

The monument is sited on a circular terrace, with broad steps that lead down

Dwight Eisenhower applauding the planned (though never built) addition to the south end of Memorial Hall

The comfortable sitting room in Memorial Hall

Memorial Hall

Minuteman Crossing

toward the Campus Pond. Gently curving walls built from local Ashfield schist provide places to sit and read, chat, or contemplate the scenery. The circular terrace surrounding the *Minuteman* statue itself, the Minuteman Crossing, is a gift from the Class of 1956 in honor of its own fiftieth reunion. The plaza is made of local Ashfield stone, a silver-gray stone that breaks into flat pieces. The stone sculpture is the product of artist John Sendelbach (a 1992 graduate of the Master of Landscape Architecture program), who also created the much-loved salamander rock sculpture in nearby Cushman Village, a work inspired by the several tunnels beneath a nearby roadway that the town of Amherst built in order to accommodate the yearly migration of salamanders seeking mates. Here as there, undulating dry-laid stone walls suggest motion; the gently arched walls surrounding the plaza slide into a series of stones laid into the grassy lawn in a spiral path, terminating in a small boulder at the center. Sendelbach conceived the initial design for this project on the UMass campus on Thanksgiving Day 2005, when he mapped its outlines on a fresh layer of snow.

11. Campus Pond
1892

Isle of View
George Trakas, 1985

The swampy lowlands of the agricultural college, between the orchards on the hillside to the east and the ridge of academic buildings to the west, were lands in between, ideal for neither campus buildings nor agricultural uses. Olmsted, in his 1866 recommendations to the Board of Trustees, urged that the Tan Brook running through this lowland area be dammed "and an ornamental pond, which will be useful for aquatic fowls and the cultivation of fish" built.[15] The dam on the northern side was built in 1892 and soon the swamp filled up with water and the Campus Pond was born. Today it is clearly the visual and emotional heart of the campus, which current students and alumni alike remember as the organizing element of the UMass campus.

Olmsted's pond landscape—the most visible remnant of Olmsted's suggestions for the campus—had as much practical value as ornamental. The water was used for the orchards, as well as ice for refrigeration, and the meadows provided hay for animals.

Isle of View and the Campus Pond

Others had more aesthetic considerations in mind. Soon after its creation, horticultural professor Samuel Maynard urged that native trees, shrubs, and herbs be planted
so that at the heart of campus would be "an artistic combination of art and nature…
a Massachusetts Garden." [16]

For students, the Campus Pond quickly became the focus of their social lives, with
autumn's fraternity initiation rituals giving way to ice skating and hockey games in
the winter and a springtime rope pull between the freshmen and sophomore classes.
More recently, rallies and celebrations found a home on the western side near the student union and under the shadow of the library, while Jazz in July and other festivals
took over the eastern side. Despite the willingness of campus leaders to give modern
architects free reign to dramatically—some would say destructively—remake the
campus landscape in the 1960s and 1970s, the Campus Pond earned the respect, and
protection, of architects, planners, and campus leaders. Pietro Belluschi, dean of MIT's
School of Architecture and architectural adviser to UMass, told a group of trustees
meeting at the offices of Sasaki Associates that the Campus Pond was an "asset of
irreplaceable value" and that the campus must protect the "visual and emotional value
of such a central landscape feature." [17] The Fine Arts Center cut off the southern
end of the pond, but that complex was intended to complement and frame the water,
and create an axis to the Campus Center on the northern end. Similarly, after toying
with the idea of putting the library directly over the pond (one option among several
discussed), Stone and campus leaders wisely chose to move it to the side. Today the
"deck" of the library overlooks the pond and frames it, as does the unfortunately undis-
tinguished Morrill buildings across the way. Together, these monumental modernist
structures help to define this campus living room. Though controversial, a classroom

facility close to Hasbrouck was redesigned in 2011 as an L-shaped building in order to avoid encroaching too much on the pond landscape (though it will disrupt the historic relationship between the Campus Center and the Fine Arts Center). Soon after the Campus Pond was constructed, the trustees, in their annual report, wrote that "simply in the light of ornamentation, it is a great addition to the college grounds." Furthermore, it "furnishes the one thing needful to make the landscape perfect—a water view."[18]

Of special note is the small island on the southern end of the Campus Pond. But what we see there today is not that island left to its own devices (there had been a small island closer to the center of the pond but erosion had washed it away by the late 1960s) but a work of art by the world-renowned landscape artist George Trakas, commissioned by the University Gallery for this site. Created between 1980 and 1985, *Isle of View* re-presents the island and the whole pond to students and faculty. Trakas built a stepped terrace that follows the curve of the south end of the pond, and he built two narrow bridges—one a massive, thirty-two-foot slab of granite and the other, a stepped metal gangway, hardly wide enough for two to pass—that led to the island. On the island (itself no more than 10 feet across and 20 feet long) Trakas created stairs leading right to the water. A few steps off the beaten paths of the campus, suddenly one finds oneself in a place of repose, a perch looking across an expanse of water. "I wanted to create a journey, a mythic trip, a natural lifeline from one half of the campus to the other," Trakas has said. "The island itself becomes a podium, a sanctuary, a place of momentary exile."[19]

Years of use and New England weather took its toll on the project. In 2006 protectors of public art on campus and nationwide banded together and, with the help of the Class of 2007's Senior Campaign, restored the piece with the help of the artist, who waded into the pond up to his waist to examine the state of his work.

12. Old Chapel
Stephen C. Earle, 1886

The symbol of the University—an "oasis in a frenetic desert," as the UMass *Daily Collegian* once wrote—the Old Chapel has served innumerable roles in its 125 years of service to the college and university.[20] It was intended, as the state Senate bill authorizing construction says, to house "a cabinet of natural history collections, a chapel for lectures and religious services, and a library and reading room."[21] Over the past century it has also been a drill hall, departmental offices for English and Mathematics, and rehearsal space for the marching band. It has been closed to the public since 1998 because of the cost of meeting current building codes. A beautiful set of carillon bells were installed in 2004, a gift of 1938 alumnus Vincent Cooper, and English Professor John Nelson, an expert in the history of clocks, assisted with needed repairs to the clockworks. Many on campus still dream of a day when the campus will once again have in the Old Chapel a glorious gathering space for important occasions.

Stephen C. Earle was Worcester's most important architect during the city's heyday of the nineteenth century. He was not as famous as his counterpart Henry Hobson

The Old Chapel

Richardson, nor perhaps as innovative, but he built dozens of significant homes and public institutions, including the Worcester Art Museum and several churches. The Old Chapel is certainly the finest example of the Richardson Romanesque in the Amherst area. As in other of Earle's buildings, and this style in general, Earle indicated the functions of the Chapel with exterior gestures: the round archives on the second floor indicate the chapel, while the regular rectangular windows on the first floor point to the building's other initial function: the college library.

The Chapel is certainly a well-bred native: it is constructed of gray Pelham granite, harvested from a quarry owned by the college. Red Longmeadow sandstone supplies the trim. The main entrance is on the east side, facing the Campus Pond. But most students and faculty see it from what was intended more as the back side—the side facing onto Hicks Way.

A four-story bell tower houses the "Old Aggie" bell, installed 1892 and dedicated in 1937 to honor entomologist Warren Elmer Hinds (1876–1936), who in 1902 earned the first PhD granted here. Above the bell tower door, a sandstone panel in the gable peak carries a high relief carving of a right arm holding a sword; this emblem of the Massachusetts State Coat of Arms (also part of the Massachusetts State Seal and the Massachusetts State Flag) symbolizes the unofficial state motto, *Ense petit*

These class years, inscribed in the base of the Chapel, mark the spots where each class once planted ivy vines.

placidam sub libertate quietem ("By the sword we seek peace, but peace only under liberty"), adopted in 1780 and affirmed as part of the great seal in 1885, the same time this building was constructed.

The affection for the Old Chapel is reflected movingly in the twenty-seven dates inscribed in the foundation stones around the base of the building. All of the graduating classes between 1900 and 1914 (and several later) had their graduating year inscribed in the stones of the Old Chapel. Here, as along the foundation of Goodell Hall, these stones mark the place where the members of these classes once planted ivy vines. The plants have long since been removed to preserve the buildings, but these inscribed stones remain to mark the gesture.

In 1916 an anonymous student lovingly reflected on the joys of the "absolute calmness" of the Chapel and its library at the center of the campus, where the quiet was only punctuated by the sounds of "baseball to west of us, bean-bags to north of us, gossip to east." [22]

13. Goodell Hall
Morse, Dickenson & Goodwin, 1934; 1959 addition, Ames and Graves

Helen Curtis Cole Commemorative Garden
1988

Today, a university library often serves as a symbol of the institution it serves, but this was not always the case. In the early history of campus libraries, these facilities were often small and housed in corners of buildings otherwise devoted to classrooms or—as was the case at UMass—shared space with a chapel. In 1849 most college libraries in New England were open just three hours a week or even less; as late as 1876, the Amherst College library across town, as was typical in that era, was open only five hours each week. But the last quarter of the century—which witnessed gathering interest in the scientific method as well as systematic and methodical approaches to policy development and social reform—saw a figurative and literal repositioning of the library as a campus institution. Libraries moved to the center of a campus's intellectual and social life, and buildings evolved accordingly, to landmark structures occupying prominent sites.

Built during this heroic moment for university libraries, Goodell Library answered this need for the campus. The college library had long outgrown its space in the 1885

Chapel across what was then still Lincoln Avenue, but it took the Great Depression and the Public Works Administration to provide enough funds (matching state investment) to make a larger library a reality. One of the biggest proponents of building a more substantial university library was Henry Hill Goodell, the college's first librarian and seventh president. He was also a central figure in what became the national Association of Land Grant Colleges and Universities, helping to advance the land grant colleges beyond their initial focus on agriculture and industry.

It also took the leadership of Hugh Baker, president during virtually the entire Massachusetts State College era. Mass Aggie became MSC in 1931; Baker took over in 1934 and stayed until 1947, when the College became the University. Baker came from New York and had held a wide range of positions in academia and industry. With his background and intellectual orientation he aspired for the new College to have a greater role on the national stage. The never-ending question of how well the Commonwealth would fund this public institution was brought to fore with the Great Depression. The federal government, which had launched the public university system with the Morrill Act, now came again to aid the public university system. With grants from the Public Works Administration, key buildings of the new college, including Goodell Library, could be built when the state was ambivalent and short of money. The College era is often forgotten, but it was a period when many of the curricular changes central to the creation of a comprehensive research university in 1947 were discussed and planned—particularly liberalizing the curriculum to include humanities and social sciences.

For the new library, Morse, Dickinson & Goodwin employed what would become the mainstay of the UMass campus for the coming three decades: a stripped-down brick Colonial Revival style, in this instance with a hip roof, cupola, and projecting two-story portico ornamented with a fan light and finished with ionic columns—the latter providing a companion for the comparably finished portico fronting Draper Hall nearby.

Goodell Hall

Today's Bernie Dallas room, a comfortable space for lectures and public events, was once a reading room in the college library.

In contrast to its successor, the 28-story Du Bois Library, the simple, even austere Goodell projects a stately appearance. The interior, too, seems designed to promote a sense of reserve. A well-appointed lobby area awash in oak paneling cultivated among visitors a scholarly demeanor. As in many libraries of this period, a bifurcated floor plan separated reading rooms from closed stacks. Today one of the most glorious of public rooms on the campus is the oak-paneled Bernie Dallas room (Dallas, '66, was a star athlete), the onetime library reading room, which constitutes the north wing of the building's main floor.

Steady growth demanded expansion, and in 1959 an addition rose to the west of the original building. Planners used the westward-sloping site to maintain the comparatively modest front facade, while accommodating a large number of books; visitors approaching the original entrance now find themselves on the fifth floor, and new stack levels extended several stories into the ground, doubling the overall space. Barely visible from the original entrance, the new wing did not enhance the building's sense of monumentality; it did, however, create a secondary, north-facing facade opposite South College that, in its emphasis on geometry and the alternating use of light and dark surfaces, resonated with the nearby Bartlett Hall that rose about the same time.

The 1959 addition on Goodell's west side on completion

Goodell lost its role as the university library when the Du Bois library opened in the early 1970s, but quickly regained it for a time during the overblown "brick crisis" that temporarily closed Du Bois. Since then it has housed various administrative offices, including the Dean of the Graduate School and Commonwealth College. It was the inadequacy of the building for an expanding Commonwealth College that led to the construction of the new honors college complex in 2012, just behind and to the south of Goodell.

Today the landscape near Goodell also includes the Helen Curtis Cole Memorial Garden, a perennial garden surrounding a granite marker that honors the life and career of the University's longtime dean of women. The second woman to serve in that role on campus, Cole (1909–2007)—Edna Skinner's successor as chief advocate for women students—came to Amherst in 1945 and saw the campus through the massive influx of the postwar period and subsequent "sexual revolution" of the late 1960s and '70s. Among other things, she was a driving force behind the creation of "Dean Helen's quad" in the Northeast Residential Area. The dean played an active role in the design and layout of these buildings, advising architects on the study and social spaces as well as kitchens and other facilities that the women students would need. The commemorative garden in her honor was designed by Meg Rasmussen—a student in the Landscape Architecture program at the time the work was installed.

14. South College

William Brocklesby, 1885; renovations, Louis Warren Ross, Boston, 1939

The Old Chapel, should it seek company from the nineteenth century, can only look out to the pond or across to South College, the last remnant of the nineteenth-century buildings built along the western ridge of the site originally dedicated to the college.

Ignoring Olmsted's advice to build a series of small buildings as needed, the College built two large buildings, South and North College, in 1866–67. North College survived until the building of Machmer Hall, just to the north. But after Old South College burned in a fire, a new building rose almost immediately, using the foundations and some walls of the destroyed building.

The 1885 South College was designed by William Brockelsby of Hartford, Connecticut, the architect of Northampton's Forbes Library as well as several buildings on the Smith and Mt. Holyoke College campuses and several churches in the Berkshires. Brocklesby attended Trinity College, graduating in 1869, and then moved to New York to study architecture with one of the foremost Gothic revivalists of the time, Richard Upjohn, architect of New York's Trinity Church and one of the founders of the American Institute of Architects. The influence of Upjohn is evident in this Gothic Revival building but hardly overwhelming. Indeed, perhaps because of the limited funds of the new college, the building has very little of the exterior detailing one would expect from a Gothic Revival building. Indeed, the *Springfield Republican* complained at the time that the exterior "treatment is plain almost to severity." [23]

Built on foundations of Pelham granite, with walls of solid Montague City bricks and adorned with trim of East Longmeadow brownstone, the building's two wings stand at right angles to one another, anchored by a picturesque tower at the southeast corner, its mansard roof and gables said to be inspired by Calvert Vaux's 1869 Belvedere Tower at New York City's Central Park. South College has always been

South College

challenging for the University. Although it is an important building both architecturally and historically, it has been remade and altered repeatedly to house multiple uses. In 1939 Louis Warren Ross remodeled the building to accommodate new activities and to make the building fireproof. The long (151 feet) but narrow wing heading west became even more of a jumble of rooms than it had been before, when it served as a dormitory.

It has housed the main offices of the president and provost as well as student dormitory rooms; the corner tower once held the student radio station, WMUA, and the meteorological observatory for the Hatch Experiment Station before that. It has sheltered a natural history collection and the school of education library. It is now home to the College of Humanities and Fine Arts, as well as the top-ranked Linguistics Department.

Perhaps as important to the history of the University as this founding building is the glorious Japanese elm that stands alongside South College. This is the first Japanese elm in the United States, brought back from Sapporo Agricultural College in Hokkaido, Japan, in 1890 by MAC Professor William Penn Brooks. The Massachusetts Agricultural College has largely disappeared from view on the UMass campus, but its founders remain heroes in Hokkaido, as the inspiration for their own college.

15. W. E. B. Du Bois Library
Edward Durrell Stone, 1973

> But in the midst of an open agricultural country, where no one can suppose abundant ground space difficult to obtain, a straight-sided, evenly-balanced, many-storied structure of stone, will not be merely incongruous to the landscape, but will certainly impose quite unnecessary inconvenience and fatigue upon those who are to occupy it.
> — *Frederick Law Olmsted, 1866* [24]

Frederick Law Olmsted just couldn't get UMass trustees to listen a hundred years earlier, when, in 1866, he urged that the campus build small, low buildings, only as many as needed at the time. A century later, as UMass was trying, belatedly, to claim its place among the greatest of public universities, the campus decided to build the tallest building in Massachusetts west of Boston and the tallest library in the world (including the two lower levels, twenty-eight stories, 297 feet tall) just steps from where the first large building that Olmsted objected to—North College—stood.

In the half century since the construction of the library in Goodell Hall, the place of libraries on college campuses had undergone yet another dramatic transformation. The rapid expansion of access to higher education launched by the G.I. Bill would have a profound effect on colleges, not simply in the exploding enrollments and consequent pressures on infrastructure, but in the very idea of the University's mission and audience, as access to a life of the mind and to the opportunities college education affords became the province of a much larger swath of the population. In order to address some of the demands those developments created, the Higher Education Facilities Act of 1963 (HEFA) offered support comprising up to one-half of a building's construction costs; by 1969 the HEFA had funded more than 600 new libraries nationwide.

The structures HEFA funded took a markedly different tack from their predecessors. Postwar thinking eschewed conformity and a preference for order and embraced instead an architectural pragmatism that favored flexibility and immediacy—or, as the 1961 issue of the *Index* called it, "simple straight angled functional construction." At the same time, the expansion of the curriculum (a process that commenced at UMass as early as the 1870s with the introduction of the "elective") in time led to specialization, and then segregation, as libraries devoted to music, art, and science emerged to serve their respective constituencies. When the new Business Administration building rose in 1964, plans included dedicated library space, while the graduate center's low-rise housed a science library, altering the role of the campus's main library.

The trustees had chosen to employ Edward Durrell Stone, one of the best-known architects of the time, because they wanted to make a mark, especially with the university library building. He understood their goals Stone was indeed one of the stars of midcentury modern architecture, the designer of embassies, corporate headquarters, and New York's Museum of Modern Art (1939). "Now, more than ever before, the Library is the heart of the University," Stone wrote in presenting his plans. "It is also a symbol of the quality of the institution itself. The size, location, and design of the building must honor the role of the Library in the University." [25]

Location had proven a topic of some debate as planners worked toward the realization of the new library. Sasaki, Dawson and Demey had recommended three possible sites for the new building. By January 1965, consensus had settled on a site directly behind (that is, to the west of) Goodell Library, but eventually planners were persuaded a site closer to the current center of campus was preferable.

Many would later accuse Stone of coasting to the finish line of his career, recycling earlier designs for this Western Massachusetts university. If this is true, Stone's initial intent was more to borrow from his American Embassy in Delhi, a low, horizontal building, than from Standard Oil in Chicago, the tower to which this library is most often compared. Former provost and chancellor Oswald Tippo recalled that when first approached about the job, Stone hoped to stretch the campus library over and around the Campus Pond. But despite all the changes to the campus in the previous decade,

The W. E. B. Du Bois Library

officials thought that alumni and students simply wouldn't stand for the decimation of the pond, the emotional core of the campus. By the time he presented his first plans, in 1966, Stone had been warned away from the pond and instead embraced a site that Sasaki Associates had identified for the library in their 1962 plan. Now he offered a design that was clearly a variation of the tower for Standard Oil in Chicago, constructed at almost exactly the same time.

The UMass library conformed to emerging trends in library design, particularly in the decision to create a tower for stacks and office space above a broad floor devoted to user services. The library's expansive main floor is below grade, conserving open space. Like the undergraduate library at the University of Illinois–Urbana (designed by Richardson, Severns, Scheeler & Associates Inc., and Clark, Altay and Associates) that rose about the same time, a courtyard visible through ample glass windows admits light and color to these underground spaces devoted to research and conversation, and is also visible from the plaza above that surrounds it, suggesting a hospitable permeability. At UMass, the courtyard's negative volume offsets the great height of the building, while the surrounding plaza, with bench seating and additional plantings, creates spaces for conversation and contemplation.

As forward looking as the structure was, in the course of the design phase, planners appeared to pull back from their instincts, which initially envisioned limestone, and chose to clad this modernist tower in brick. Stone insisted he was agnostic as to the choice of cladding. Writing to President Lederle in 1969, Stone wrote, "I wish I could be more decisive in the choice of the exterior material for our building. In fairness, the design lends itself to either limestone or brick. Therefore, it is a matter of relating it to the existing and future buildings. As the campus exists in its present state, perhaps the brick would be more harmonious. However, you may consider with the advent of the Saarinen building [Kevin Roche's Fine Arts Center] at one end of the open area and the Breuer building at the other [the Campus Center], both of grayish concrete, that the library should harmonize with the new modern buildings on the campus." [26]

In the end, the decision was less about whether the University would project an avant-garde look or a more traditional one. It may simply have been about money. The building was already looking to be well over budget even before the "great concrete pour" on April 21, 1969, which launched construction. Limestone would have cost close to a million dollars more than brick and would have required removing several floors from the building. Special Assistant to the Provost David Clay, who had been centrally involved in the design process, put it succinctly: "I am convinced that a larger build-ing in brick will serve the university's needs better than a squat tower in limestone." [27] Provost Tippo took the question to the Faculty Senate. The vote was overwhelming: the faculty wanted the height (and so capacity) retained.

The end result was an icon, visible from miles away, that provided a clear center to the University. The tower was organized with a central core of high-speed eleva-tors and quiet floors with little foot traffic, as is common in low-rise libraries. Students and faculty would be treated to many quiet spaces around the stacks, with spec-tacular views on all sides, to the Pelham Hills, the Holyoke Range, and the Berkshire Mountains. Like the towers in Southwest, which were intended as a series of stacked "houses," the library was imagined by Stone as a series of alternating floors, with ware-house floors sandwiched between floors for seminar rooms and carrels for students and faculty in fields related to the nearby books. The plan was never fully imple-mented, but the uniform appearance from the outside belies a varied set of functions on different floors. In 1875 the university library consisted of five hundred volumes. When it opened the Du Bois Library was the anchor of a library system of over a million volumes. Today the library consists of eight million books, periodicals, maps, and other collections and has burst the bounds of even this massive structure: a good portion of the UMass library collection lies within the bowels of the Holyoke Range, in a former Cold War–era bunker (a 1957 Strategic Air Command facility that, for many visitors, still conjures images from *Dr. Strangelove*) concealed within Bare Mountain that today serves as the Five College Book Depository.

It was the bricks, however, that would detract from an appreciation of the library's many impressive features. The massive piers rising the full height of the building emphasize the building's height, but almost as soon as the building opened, brick frag-ments began to fall from the tower. In 1979, fearing that the problem was worse than just chipping, the campus administration closed the library for the entire fall semes-ter and 250,000 books were taken back to Goodell, the old college library building. Accusations between architect, engineer, and builder flew—had the architect and engineer failed to account for the weight of the 30-foot stacks of brick when designing the angle irons holding them in place? Had the engineer failed to calculate the outward

pull? Had the builder simply failed to construct the facade well enough? All of these questions were asked more urgently because of the very real bricks that fell from the scandal-ridden building of the UMass Boston campus at Columbia Point in Dorchester. The flawed construction (which continues to undermine that massive complex to this day) and the bribes to elected leaders brought down Senate majority leader Joseph J.C. DiCarlo of Revere and several other legislative leaders. The problem at UMass was never so severe, and ultimately, the issue was deemed to be minor: a limited number of bricks, at the relieving angles spaced along each side of the library, had been cut back to narrow the mortar joints, thereby making them more susceptible to chipping from the freeze and thaw cycle. The library was reopened before the end of the academic year and years later a campus fund-raising campaign replaced the initial chain-link fence with a more permanent but less obtrusive barrier—but the UMass Amherst library got swept up in the image of a scandal-plagued state procurement system. Unfortunately, the urban legend of bricks regularly falling on students' heads persists. (Other urban legends have accompanied the library, such as one asserting that the architect never accounted for the weight of the books in his designs. That story in particular has no basis in fact and is routinely repeated about any number of university libraries.)

If falling shards of brick were not enough, controversy erupted two decades later when the trustees were pushed by activist students and faculty to rename the building—to date called simply the "tower library"—after one of Massachusetts's most influential sons, born and bred in Great Barrington. "As we march into the Twenty-First Century," wrote the trustees, "we feel that it is time to go beyond the color line and appropriately name the tower library in honor of one of the finest heroes, not only of Massachusetts but of the world—William Edward Burghardt Du Bois." [28] The decision was applauded by many but decried by others who saw Du Bois as a communist who had given up his U.S. citizenship to live his last years in Ghana. (Du Bois did not give up his citizenship; the U.S. government had denied him a new passport when he lived in Ghana. He was indeed sympathetic to communism because of its critique of capitalism and its insistent acceptance of all races.) Today, one of the finest collections of Du Bois papers can be viewed in the University Archives, on the twenty-fifth floor. Looking west from the top of the library, one can almost see to Great Barrington, where Du Bois grew up. The University owns the boyhood home site of this seminal figure and has been conducting archaeological field schools here for years; today, faculty and community members are making it a memorial and interpretive site.

Today, the courtyard contains the Oswald Tippo Library Courtyard and Sculpture Garden, named for former provost and botany professor Oswald Tippo. As provost under President John W. Lederle beginning in 1964, he had overseen much of the University's transformation. The space is dominated by artist Thomas Matsuda's work *Searching for the Buddha in the Mountains*. Installed in 1999, the piece assembles pine sculptures of varying height, from 2 to 8 feet, each with a hand-chiseled surface, in a constellation inspired by the rocks in Japanese dry gardens. The series of sculpted wooden forms deploys a traditional Japanese technique, *yosegi tsukuri*; this process of hollowing, pinning, and joining has been used in the creation of Buddhist

The library courtyard contains a garden as well as Thomas Matsuda's sculptural installation Searching for the Buddha in the Mountains. *South College and Thompson Hall are visible in the background.*

A comparatively recent addition to the campus center landscape is this garden on its north side, a gift of the Class of 1955.

statues for centuries. Nine carved wooden abstract forms allude, the artist notes, "to mountains / rocks / people / spirits / Buddhas." [29] Matsuda's work seeks "to synthesize Eastern and Western cultures, bringing together aspects of both—freedom and discipline, tradition and change, ritual and openness, spirituality and materialism" to "create something new that goes beyond either." Created with the help of the Stockbridge School and the Physical Plant, the garden surrounding the artwork is today maintained by a dedicated team of library staff and student volunteers.

More recently, a second garden space north of the building has transformed the building's setting once again. Funded by the Class of 1955 and installed by the architecture firm Edwards & Kelcey, this 2005 addition to campus addressed a need for better access to the building while creating an attractive garden landscape by providing two long intersecting ramps just west of the existing monumental staircase that fill the slope between the library's north elevation and the Student Union beyond. At the intersection, a low semicircular stone wall provides ample seating around a central courtyard surrounded by a terraced garden.

16. Machmer Hall
James A. Britton, 1957

Thompson Hall
James A. Britton, 1968

If the Whitmore Administration building marks one end of Hicks Way, Machmer Hall marks the other. Syracuse-trained architect James A. Britton's contribution to campus was constructed in 1957 adjacent to North College, one of the college's first buildings; indeed old North survived for a few years after the creation of Machmer before

The Thompson tower beside the low-lying Machmer Hall

finally being demolished. Machmer—a 73,000-square-foot departmental and classroom building originally built for the Mathematics Department (and now housing Sociology, Anthropology, and Communications)—is a U-shaped building, with two wings built north of the three-story front. It is part of a trio of buildings constructed in sequence—with Hasbrouck Hall (1950) and the Student Union (also 1957)—that settled the architectural look of the campus until another trio of structures (the Lincoln Campus Center, the Fine Arts Center, and the Du Bois Library) changed the skyline of the campus once again. Hasbrouck Hall and the Student Union fulfilled two important needs in the postwar boom and the transformation of the College into the University of Massachusetts: more classroom space and a gathering place for students and their organizations. Underneath the skin of Machmer is a structure just like those of the new dormitories rising up to the east of North Pleasant Street. But on the outside, the new university was making a statement, if only tentatively, and only in its nonresidential buildings. In many ways, the stylistic choice (which can be seen in a number of buildings, such as Bartlett Hall) was a modest step toward modernism. Unwilling to abandon the red brick of earlier buildings and the model of Amherst College, the young University nonetheless gravitated toward a popular stripped-down style, looking in both directions, forward and backward, at once.

Machmer's semicircular exterior stair on the east side was designed with Olmsted (Ellis) Drive in mind. The nineteenth-century road passed right in front of the building, curving in front of the Student Union, as it made its way past the future site of the Campus Center and back to North Pleasant Street. The building is named for William Lawson Machmer (1899–1953), one of the longest-serving administrators in UMass's history. Machmer served under five presidents across forty-two years, and his tenure at the University as professor and dean spanned the MAC, MSC, and UMass eras.

Just to the west of Machmer and attached by an enclosed passage is Britton's Thompson Hall (1968). A one-story building, overlooking the steeply sloping hill to what were once the fields, holds several large lecture halls, while the tower is largely faculty offices. As the University expanded rapidly in the 1950s and '60s, dormitories, classrooms, and laboratories came first. Thompson was built largely to answer the crushing need for faculty offices. Being able to offer private offices was seen as essential to the recruitment of a top-flight faculty; at the same time, as administrators wrote during the planning of the building, faculty would have no excuses to work at home and instead could be expected to be seen on campus for most of the day.

The Student Union

17. Student Union
Louis Warren Ross, 1957

The failure of plans to dramatically expand Memorial Hall after World War II in order to honor World War II veterans and turn it into a student activities center only accentuated the need for such a center. In 1957 the rapidly growing university built this 106,000-square-foot building right along Ellis (Olmsted) Way. As the largest building project to that time, housing student organizations, a bowling alley, and restaurants, the Student Union was a sign of the rapid growth of the campus, and the shift to a comprehensive research and teaching university, with student extracurricular activities seen as central to their educational experience.

The name *university* came in 1947, but the campus was hardly prepared for the rapid influx of students. Draper Commons, just to the north, was the only dining hall and even then it could not handle the 3,220 students of the growing university. President Ralph Van Meter launched a $7 million building program in 1948 that aimed to double student capacity. The Student Center was essential as well. After some debate as to the site, it was decided that this site was most easily reached by foot from the new dormitories under construction.

The architect of the Student Union was the largely unknown Louis Warren Ross, an active alumnus and a member of the institution's UMass alumni corporation, which formed in the mid-1930s. He opened his Boston firm in 1935 and from that time until the early 1960s, he became the most prolific architect of the campus. He would be responsible for the design of more than thirty structures, including nearly all the dormitories constructed between 1935 and 1963. This body of work established the Georgian Revival style as a dominant tradition for the residential quadrangles of the campus. However, Ross's work for the school would also include Skinner Hall (1948), the Lincoln Apartments (1949), and the Student Union, the latter designed in the new, more modernist-inflected style of the post-war era.

The Student Union is distinguished by its large, two-story glazed bay on the west elevations. Polished granite square columns give the building a feeling of reserved grandeur similar to other public buildings, while the curved windows of the Cape Cod lounge allude to the nautical motifs common in "moderne" architecture of the time. The exterior columns are of gray and green marble, while Deco grilles enliven the facade (and echo those on Machmer, across the way). The large curved front wall with a grid of square windows was a dramatic welcome to passersby on Ellis Way, which still crossed in front of the building when it opened. Inside is a two-story atrium leading to a large ballroom with extensive glazing that provides views out to the Pond and Metawampe Lawn. With the toll of time and the thousands who flow through this building every day, it can take a moment to appreciate the richness of the design. The ballroom itself was an opulent gathering place for major campus events. The wall of windows and terrace frame the eastern side, while six feet of wood wainscoting wraps the entire space and fluted pilasters mark the stage. The ballroom was used for cultural events, though its challenging acoustics later proved another justification for the massive Fine Arts Center project.

The Student Union contained the Hatchet and Pipe—its name an unfortunate remnant of popular misunderstandings of Native American–European contact in New England—a lively campus bar and restaurant. It is now a food court known as The Hatch. The Union is also home to the People's Market and Earthfoods Café,

The lobby space of the Student Union

enterprises that capture the distinct UMass spirit. The People's Market was launched in 1973 by Ellen Gavin and Gail Sullivan, 19-year-olds who bonded during their freshman year when both of them joined the takeover of the ROTC building. In founding the market, the activists sought to create a nonprofit, community-owned grocery store that would stock healthy, affordable food—issues that continue to resonate on the campus today. Three years later, like-minded students founded the Earthfoods Café, a vegetarian collective. Today Earthfoods serves between 400 and 500 people each day in the Student Union's Commonwealth Room.

The south side of the building has a terrace with views to the Campus Pond, and is a popular place for student events, including political rallies. Indeed, the Student Union has proven to be the gathering point for many campus political events, with speakers and their causes choosing the front (west) entrance, the terrace, or the ballroom inside, to make their arguments heard. If one of UMass's distinguishing features over the past half century has been the political activism of its faculty and students, the Student Union has been the place where that activism has been most visibly expressed.

18. Murray D. Lincoln Campus Center and Parking Garage
Marcel Breuer and Associates, 1970

This tour of the central campus culminates with the first of the three great modernist monuments in the center of campus, the Murray D. Lincoln Campus Center, designed by Marcel Breuer. Built in 1970, the Campus Center was soon followed by the Du Bois Library and the Fine Arts Center, creating an outdoor exhibition of midcentury modern architecture.

Breuer was one of the central figures of the Bauhaus school in Germany in the 1920s, but fled to London, and then the United States, with the rise of the Nazis

Marcel Breuer's Campus Center, one of the three midcentury modern buildings that define the center of campus

(Breuer was of Hungarian-Jewish descent). Many offices around the world unwittingly showcase Breuer's design innovations—his metal-tube Cesca and Wasilly chairs are icons of modernist design. But he is best known for his later works of Brutalist architecture—aggressive, concrete sculptural projects. His most famous project, completed just as he began designing the Campus Center, is the Whitney Museum of American Art (1966) on the Upper East Side of Manhattan. For the Campus Center project, and most of his other significant buildings in the 1950s and '60s, Breuer worked closely with his partner, Herbert Beckhard.

The Campus Center is an eleven-story multiuse behemoth. Several stories underground are meeting rooms; the offices of the *Daily Collegian,* the campus newspaper; other student organizations; and a spectacular, cavelike auditorium for major events. On the concourse level is a bustling hall including the University Store and restaurants (like the Blue Wall—once among the Valley's best-known live music venues). The tower consists of 116 hotel guest rooms, 36 conference meeting rooms, administrative offices, and, at the top, the Marriott Center for Hospitality Management, part of the Isenberg School of Management. (It was once the Top of the Campus restaurant.) Visitors can enter the building directly from the parking garage through the underground passageway, and the complex is intentionally connected to the lowest level of the Student Union, a building that quickly outgrew its capacities in the 1960s and 1970s.

Breuer's design successfully framed Metawampe Lawn to the south of the building and east of the Student Union. It remains a popular place for outdoor gatherings and other campus events. But the most striking, and for many the least successful, gesture was to raise the visible part of the building up onto a platform, dozens of steps up from the lawn. The tower of the campus center now floats above a broad expanse. The plaza on the north side of the building is interrupted by pyramidal skylights designed to admit light to the cavernous concourse and ballroom levels below. And the huge wall of glass

Below grade, the campus center auditorium accommodates 660 guests.

The lobby of the Campus Center

in the hotel lobby is an impressive sight, sandwiched as it is between the broad concrete plaza and nine floors of the weighty building above. But the plaza itself remains an underused, often windswept space, unlike the platform of the Du Bois library, which, by virtue of it serving as a pathway across campus, is much more active.

The Campus Center did not fare well among critics when it opened. Jane Holtz Kay, writing in the *Boston Globe,* called it a "honeycomb fortress…on stilts." [30] Campus magazines jokingly asked, "Waffles, anyone?" in reference to the grid of concrete openings. More recently, renovations to the hotel and conference rooms in the tower gave a cleaner look to the building but also removed some of Breuer's designs.

Like other modernist structures on campus, the building has slowly gained defenders. For one, the building works well in conjunction with the Fine Arts Center and the Du Bois Library to frame the Campus Pond landscape and was key to giving the campus a visual core. But the building itself deserves a closer look to appreciate its complexity. Breuer made what could have been a simple rectangular block of a building into a proud piece of sculpture. The nine-story stairwells on both ends break up the rigidity of a rectilinear facade, and the use of multiple fenestration patterns employed to distinguish the different uses—hotel, meeting, and conference rooms—make for a lively public face, especially on the less frequently seen north-facing side. Huge floor slabs are marked with lines so that floors and functions are made obvious.

Marcel Breuer's Campus Center Garage

Light pierces the latticework of the Campus Center parking garage.

As with the Du Bois Library, some of the Campus Center's best attributes are the views it affords of the campus and the whole region. Looking south from the eleventh floor of Marriott Conference Center, the church spires of the town and college are visible—Johnson Chapel at Amherst College, the Grace Episcopal Church, and St. Brigid's Catholic Church. To the north and west, one can see Mt. Greylock, the tallest mountain in Massachusetts, and Mt. Monadnock in southern New Hampshire. To the northeast is visible another religious building, of a different kind: the white dome of the Buddhist Peace Pagoda in the Leverett Hills. Finally, up on Clark Hill to the east, town and gown are joined together, with the Georgian tower of Van Meter Hall and the town's water towers standing side by side.

An especially intriguing part of the Campus Center design is the parking garage, which continues the grid theme of the Campus Center and makes for an unexpectedly grand backdrop to the eastern entrance to the Campus Center concourse. The light shining through the concrete grid screen enlivens an otherwise mundane arrival sequence.

An interior courtyard contains two works of public art: Jonathan Kohrman's 1989 outdoor mural *Civility*, an acrylic on plyboard work that aims to promote the "goals of the university community to live and work together with cooperation, enthusiasm and joy," alongside ceramicist and sculptor Brenda Minisci's 1971 fiberglass fountain piece *Fiore Verdi* (a gift of the Class of 1970). The mural emerged from a design com-

petition launched by the departments of Landscape Architecture & Regional Planning, Afro-American Studies, and Art; UMass students modeled for the work, which, as a panel at the installation explains, "portrays enrichment through participation in a multiculturally diverse University."

The Center is named for alumnus Murray D. Lincoln, a national leader in consumer and producer cooperatives and founder and president of CARE from 1945 to '57.

Brenda Minisci's Fiore Verdi *(1971)*

19. Metawampe Lawn and Metawampe Sculpture
Randolph Wardell Johnston, 1950

On the south lawn of the Campus Center, east of the Student Union, is a bronze statue dedicated to Chief Metawampe. The five-foot-eight-inch figure, dressed in a fringed breech cloth and wearing two feathers in his long, braided hair, holds a musket in one hand and a powder horn in the other. The granite pedestal beneath reads, "METAWAMPE, Legendary Spirit of the Redmen. Given by the Class of 1950, Erected by the Class of 1956."

Originally mounted on a granite boulder below the northeast corner of the Old Chapel, the statue dates from the era when the school's athletic teams were the "Redmen." Chief Metawampe alludes to a historical figure associated with the seventeenth-century arrival of English immigrants to this section of the Connecticut Valley. Evidence of Metawampe as a symbol of the campus comes as early as 1907,

Metawampe

when faculty and staff formed an outing group called the Metawampe Club, which took annual hikes over local mountains, including the College-owned Mt. Toby. Metawampe was formally made a symbol of the UMass campus in 1948, and the Class of 1950 commissioned this work shortly thereafter. Canadian (and later Bahamian) sculptor Randolph Wardell Johnston was a professor of art at Smith College when he cast this work.

In time, the statue—which some came to find an offensive caricature of native culture—attracted vandalism. The work was moved to its current location in 1956 and today stands atop a circular platform, nestled among a bank of rhododendrons.

1 Patricia Wright, "Name that Style: Robsham Center by Any Other Name is Architectural Attraction," press release from UMass News Office, May 22, 1989.
2 "Business Administration, School of," RG36, Series 101, Box 13, Special Collections and University Archives (SCUA).
3 Robert Campbell, "A Prototype, but Never to Be Repeated," *Boston Globe*, January 6, 1974.
4 The UMass Amherst yearbook, *Index* (1975), 70.

5   William Venman to President John Lederle, December 8, 1964, Academic Affairs/Tippo, Box 1 f. 17, SCUA.

6   Kevin Roche, interview with Max Page, Hampden, Conn., November 1, 2011.

7   Philip Bezanson to Dean I. Mcyer Hunsberger, September 24, 1964, Academic Affairs/Tippo, Box 2 f. 5, SCUA.

8   "The University Museum of Contemporary Arts Bringing The World to UMass Amherst," last modified February 23, 2011, http://blogs.umass.edu/lbp/2011/02/23/ the-university-museum-of-contemporary-arts-bringing-the-world-to-umass-amherst.

9   Inaugural Program, 1975, RG36, series 101, Box 7, SCUA.

10 *Artist & fabricator: exhibition held at the Fine Arts Center Gallery, University of Massachusetts/ Amherst, September 23–November 9, 1975* (Amherst: Fine Arts Center Gallery, University of Massachusetts, 1975), 13.

11 Michael Abrahamson, "Brutalism: The Word Itself and What We Mean When We Say It," November 20, 2011, http://criticundertheinfluence.wordpress.com/2011/11/20 /brutalism-the-word-itself-and-what-we-mean-when-we-say-it/.

12 Design booklet, RG 36, series 101, Box 1A, folder 3, SCUA.

13 "Cornerstone," RG 36, series 101, Box 1A, folder 1, SCUA.

14 "UMass Class of 1950 to Dedicate Minuteman Statue Oct. 12 Across from Campus Pond," press release from UMass News Office, October 10, 2002.

15 Frederick Law Olmsted, "A Few Things to be Thought of Before Proceeding to Plan Buildings for the National Agricultural Colleges," in *The Papers of Frederick Law Olmsted: The Years of Olmsted, Vaux, and Co., 1865–74* (Baltimore: Johns Hopkins University Press, 1992), 132.

16 Segments of Campus, Campus Pond and Isle of View, RG 36, Series 104, "Histories," SCUA.

17 Minutes, Trustee Committee on Building and Grounds, November 14, 1963, held at the Sasaki office.

18 13th Annual Report of the Massachusetts Agricultural College, January 1893. Public Document no. 31, 115.

19 "Improving the View," last modified March 13, 2009, http://www.umass.edu/umhome/feature-story/ article/14.

20 "Oasis in a Frenetic Desert," *Daily Collegian*, September 27, 1971.

21 "Chapel—Resolutions 1884–1888," RG36, Series 101, Box 12, SCUA.

22 Anonymous, "The Creation of a Library Atmosphere," (1916), 36, 101, 12, "Chapel—news clippings, 1882," SCUA.

23 *Springfield Republican*, October 18, 1885, Group 36, Box 13, series 101 folder "South College, 1885, 1967, 1977."

24 Olmsted, "A Few Things to be Thought of…," 140.

25 "Architects Proposal, ca 1966," 8/5/3 Box 43, folder 1, SCUA.

26 Edward Durrell Stone to President John Lederle, October 31, 1967, RG8 8 5,3 Folder 29 SCUA.

27 David Clay to President Lederle, December 4, 1967, RG8 8 5,3 Folder 29, SCUA.

28 Trustee Document Tc4-096, SCUA.

29 Thomas Matsuda artist's statement, "Searching for the Buddha in the Mountains," http://www.tmatsuda.com/statmnt_serchbud.html.

30 Jane Holtz Kay, "The UMass Campus: A Passing Mark?" *Boston Globe*, September 20, 1970,

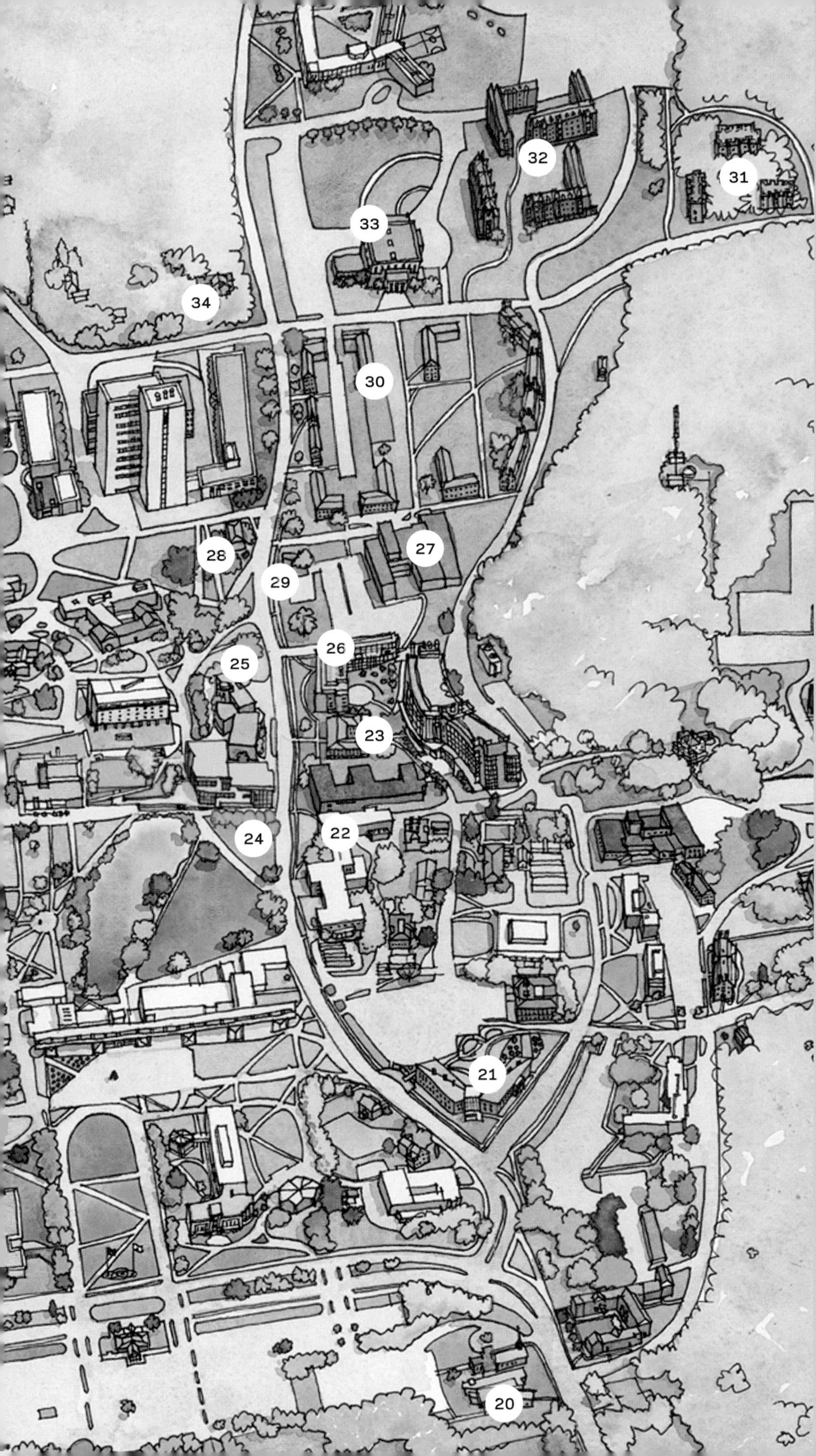

32
31
33
34
30
27
28
29
26
25
23
24
22
21
20

Walk Two: North Pleasant Street

North Pleasant Street—not to be confused with East Pleasant Street, which runs nearly parallel, along the other side of Clark Hill—was created along with the campus itself, as an alternative to an older roadway, Stockbridge Road, just east along the ridge. Campus planners felt that the existing route north from Amherst to Sunderland couldn't accommodate the needs of the school, so in January 1866 county commissioners met to lay out a new roadway just to the west; North Pleasant Street was completed the following October.

The name Pleasant Street is associated both with Mt. Pleasant—the southern tip of the ridge that today defines the eastern edge of campus—and the Mount Pleasant Institution (also known as the Mt. Pleasant Classical Institute), a large Greek Revival building that from the late 1820s housed a school for boys. The school closed in 1836 and the large wings were detached and repurposed—one becoming a tenement on this road known locally as "the beehive." All that remains of the school today is the name of North Pleasant Street.

At the end of the nineteenth century, the agricultural college was linked to the wider world through a street railway. In 1896 the Amherst and Sunderland Street Railway was chartered, with Walter D. Cowls as president; it began operations in the summer of 1897. Eight miles of track led through the length of Amherst. In 1900 the line was connected to Northampton. Buses and cars largely replaced the trolleys and by the 1950s, the last rails were pulled up. Until 2012 all that remained of the trolley line was the waiting station near Hasbrouck Hall, and it was razed in June of that year.

Ironically, this main thoroughfare, on which many of the earliest buildings were built, never became the main artery of campus life. When UMass was founded in 1863 there was no Campus Pond, and no educational buildings flanked North Pleasant Street. Campus development would occur along Stockbridge Road, between what are now Wilder and French Halls. The first college buildings to appear alongside what

This view looking east from the playing fields where Haigis Mall now sits captures a glimpse of the southern end of North Pleasant street in the early twentieth century.

East Experiment Station is one of the oldest buildings extant along North Pleasant Street; Skinner Hall and the Northeast Residential Area are visible as the street continues north.

is today North Pleasant Street were the East and West Experiment Stations, constructed in the 1880s, and they would find few companions in the years to come.

As late as 1919, then, travelers along North Pleasant Street looking east would have seen market garden plots and the backs of Wilder Hall and the Stockbridge house, and looking west would have seen a broad expanse across the pond to the Chapel. The construction of the Abigail Adams house (later destroyed by fire) just north of the West Experiment Station was the first major construction of the twentieth century.

It was not until after World War II that academic buildings began to fill in along North Pleasant Street, with the Physics and Home Economics buildings (Hasbrouck and Skinner halls) in 1947 and the 1950s. Next came the large residential complex called Northeast—Hamlin, Arnold, and Knowlton (the latter named for Assistant Professor of Rural Home Life Helen Knowlton, responsible for transforming the Homestead—which at that time stood across the street—into a practice facility for the Home Economics students) along North Pleasant, with Leach and Crabtree behind and then followed by the massive Morrill Science Center, the Fine Arts Center, and the Lederle Graduate Research Center. The Roman Catholic Diocese built the Newman Center in 1963 at the prominent intersection of North Pleasant Street and Massachusetts Avenue. More recently, the North Pleasant corridor has been filled in with the Integrated Sciences Building and Graham Gund's Studio Arts Building.

The gradual "occupation" of North Pleasant Street by the campus led to numerous calls—including the 1953 campus plan—to close off the roadway to through traffic and make it a pedestrian mall. Hideo Sasaki renewed the proposal in the 1960s as part of a general effort to redirect traffic, and while he succeeded in closing the route along the west side of the pond to automobiles (Hicks Way), North Pleasant street proved more politically challenging. The call to close the street was reissued in the 2012 campus plan. Other elements of the University's vision also reach out along North Pleasant Street, including a gateway development district that envisions a walkable transition zone between the campus and downtown Amherst.

Gordon Hall

20. Gordon Hall
Miller Pollin Architects, 2003

In the founding years of the agricultural college, the land bordering campus to the south was residential, with several buildings around North Pleasant and Fearing Streets over time housing fraternities. By 1947 a dozen fraternities and sororities stood between Fearing Street and Butterfield Terrace. Heading into the belly of the beast, in 1964 the

Gordon Hall atrium

First Baptist Church left its 1838 building (which still stands on the Common in downtown Amherst) and chose another site adjacent to the campus.

Campus reached back. In 2003 Gordon Hall, a 24,000-square-foot building located on a privately owned site next door to the Baptist Church, became home to PERI, the Political Economy Research Institute, as well as several UMass departments. Designed by Sigrid Miller Pollin, a faculty member in the Architectural + Design program of the UMass Department of Art, Architecture and Art History, the building's two three-story wings, inspired in part by the tobacco barns that are

The Northeast Residential complex (foreground) sits across Eastman Lane from Totman Gymnasium (left) and the North Residential Area; the Sylvan Residential Area is visible in the distance.

a distinctive building type in the Connecticut River Valley, are angled toward one another to create a double-height, triangular central atrium space. The exterior cedar siding challenges the institutional feel by turning away from the conventional materials—brick, concrete, steel—of UMass buildings. The motive in each of these design choices was to open up the traditional academic building and create a gathering space for faculty and students from different fields. Symbolically, the wings of these buildings also speak to the merging of "town and gown" at this site, which straddles the campus and the larger community.

21. Studio Arts Building
Gund Partnership, 2008

On a campus that notoriously lacks any clear gateway, Graham Gund's 52,881-gross-square-foot Studio Arts Buildings does its best to create one. Located at a key intersection, where North Pleasant Street and Stockbridge Road split, the building accentuates the dramatic corner. The V-shaped plan is organized around a two-story atrium that provides exhibition, lecture, and social space, augmented by glowing neon, which runs through a cycle of colors. The two wings contain a mix of faculty offices, studios, and seminar rooms. Due to cost considerations the atrium space was almost eliminated as superfluous, but without it, the building would have lost much of its distinction, and students and faculty a unique gathering space. Another late decision made by the then chancellor John Lombardi was to clad the building in brick, something not contemplated by the architects, who envisioned a metal cladding. In this example of the ongoing struggle between the avant-garde and the more traditional, the latter won out. The Studio Arts Building is the latest in what we might call the "rebrickification" of the UMass campus, after a modernist interlude in the 1960s and '70s.

The Studio Arts Building

Graham Gund is one of a number of architects trained by Walter Gropius in the international style who later embraced historic preservation and postmodern historicist designs. Designer of the Hyatt Regency Cambridge (1976), with its references to the Viennese modernist Adolf Loos, and the Boston Architectural College (also 1976), in the Brutalist mode of the Boston City Hall and UMass's Fine Arts Center, Gund also designed the 75 State Street Tower in Boston (1989) and several projects for the Walt Disney Company in both Florida and California, all of which embraced ornament and traditional forms once again.

The building unites programs and studios that were dispersed across the campus, often in repurposed agricultural buildings, such as the Munson Hall Annex, which briefly housed sculpture studios. The ends of the building may appear almost severe. They were designed with the possibility of expansion in mind. The parking lot behind the building has long been eyed for new construction.

22. Morrill Science Center

James H. Ritchie Associates, Morris W. Maloney, and Desmond and Lord, 1959–66

The Morrill Science Center—erected in stages, with Morrill I rising in 1959, II in 1960, III in 1963, and IV in 1966—was built to house teaching and research space for natural sciences departments, including Biology, Geology, Microbiology, and Zoology. Today the completed building constitutes one of the largest structures on campus. Sited prominently, high and opposite the Campus Pond, Morrill has an oversized, three-story glazed entrance that foreshadowed the architectural vocabulary of much later in the century. But the bulk of the building is an effort (less than successful, most would say) to harmonize the neo-Georgian brick dormitories further north along the street and east up Clark Hill, and the modern inflections of the buildings of the 1950s and '60s.

Morrill Science Center

Part of the problem is that the building was erected over sixteen years (with further major renovations coming early in the new century and continuing today), by three different architects. James H. Ritchie Associates, the architects of the very different and more successful Memorial Hall, designed the western entranceway. The southern wing was the product of Desmond and Lord and the wings that straddle an exterior passageway were by Morris W. Maloney, architect of Boyden Gym and the Worcester Dining Commons. The interior is equally challenging, as the four buildings-within-a-building are nearly impossible to navigate; today, hand-drawn maps posted years ago still guide students through the labyrinth that is Morrill. The later wings, however, are not totally without charm: the exterior east-west passageway frames the Du Bois Library perfectly.

23. Skinner Hall
Louis Warren Ross, 1948; renovation, Anshen+Allen+Rothman, 2006

Food shortages during World War II had prompted interest in education for women in fields such as home economics. When the Massachusetts Agricultural College launched its program in 1918, President Kenyon Butterfield hired Edna L. Skinner to direct the department. Skinner served as professor and adviser of women from 1919 to 1946 and became first dean of the School of Home Economics in 1945.

During World War II, the number of female students doubled. Many of these young women enrolled in the home economics program, eventually housed in Skinner Hall. Designed by architect Louis Warren Ross (a member of the College's Class of 1917) to serve as the first structure designed specifically for this field of study, this three-story brick Georgian Revival building, sited at the top of a small embankment, continued the use of mostly Georgian Revival architectural details, which Ross had previously employed in his designs for residential buildings. In another gesture toward the domestic, Ross purposefully alluded, in the massive surround of the building's entrance, to the distinct Connecticut Valley doorways—among the region's most

Skinner Hall

An interpretation of the iconic Connecticut River Valley doorway

recognizable architectural forms. The iconic scrolled pediment, the fluted pilasters topped with rosettes and pedestal moldings of the mid-eighteenth century all linked the modern building with old residential forms long known in the Valley. Roof balustrades, raking cornices with applied dentils, a semicircular light in the gable, and massive brick chimneys designed to appear as four-flue chimneys all complete and complement the allusion to domestic gentility.

Skinner Hall and the Student Union were the only nonresidential structures Ross designed for the campus. The commission was made even as Ross was completing work for the Central and Northeast residential districts. When growing female enrollment made new facilities necessary, this site, convenient to the female housing district, was chosen. (Although initially planned for male dormitories, the Northeast district was in time allocated for female housing.) Edna Skinner, who had lobbied for years for the construction of a dedicated site for the home economics program, retired just before her namesake building would be completed.

The building was substantially altered during a 2006–9 rehabilitation when it was renovated to house the School of Nursing. The interior was completely gutted, and the original divided light wood sash windows replaced with conventional fixed and double-hung sash. A significant addition—a two-story 11,600-square-foot wing housing a hospital instruction lab, examination lab, and hospital simulation suites—filled in the building's original rear court. Campus designers used the renovations of Skinner, which required making the building accessible to people with disabilities, to transform the pathway into the building. The historic entry steps and plantings were removed and a new ramp and dynamic, asymmetric stair were built.

These changes make for a fascinating and largely successful combination of old and new. Ross's neo-Georgian facade still reigns on the hillside, but the building's modern additions give the building a contemporary energy. The bright open windows, off-center stair, and sharply angled additions just visible from North Pleasant Street speak of new facilities and new activities. Given that the campus is hardly short on fine neo-Georgian buildings—many by Ross—it seems altogether appropriate to welcome this innovative variation on a theme.

The final word in this dialogue between past and present is the tall, lone elm tree, which has managed to survive through an almost complete change to its environment.

This view shows the waiting station as well as the trolley lines that passed along what was then largely a rural country lane.

24. Waiting Station
Arthur Sharpe, 1911

Across the street from Skinner Hall, near the south corner of Hasbrouck Hall, once stood a waiting station designed by Arthur Sharpe (Class of 1910) as a practicum in a landscape course. This brick and stucco structure, which featured a low-grade hip roof that extended out over paired brackets, synthesized Italianate- and Craftsman-style design elements, and was designed to allow views out in all directions for travelers waiting for the next trolley. In 2012, as this book was in production, a new classroom building project, which will wrap around the south and west sides of Hasbrouck Hall, resulted in the unplanned of the waiting station.

25. Hasbrouck Hall and Hasbrouck Laboratory
Kilham, Hopkins, Greeley, and Brodie, 1950;
with additions by Desmond and Lord, 1964

Hasbrouck Laboratory was constructed in 1947 to house the Department of Physics, founded in 1911 by Philip Bevier Hasbrouck. The building's chief architect was William Roger Greeley, who designed it to complement, but also move beyond, nearby Skinner Hall and the other neo-Georgian buildings dominating the campus. The building is not parallel to North Pleasant Street; rather, it angles away to the east, perhaps in defer-ence to the ending of Ellis Way (which began a quarter mile south on North Pleasant Street by the Studio Arts Building) between Hasbrouck and West Experiment Station.

The 1964 Hasbrouck Hall, a later addition to Hasbrouck Laboratory, upon construction

Hasbrouck Laboratory has been called the first significant modern structure on the institution's campus. It was a leap forward from the aging wooden building that still sheltered physics at UMass despite the advent of the Atomic Age. Although the building's construction technology (concrete and steel frame) conformed to other projects of the period, Greeley's exterior form departed decisively from the Georgian Revival style influencing dormitory construction. Such a distinction was not uncommon to post–World War II campus architecture, when science facilities often embraced the symbolic connotations of modern design, while residential construction adopted the Georgian vernacular.

The lab's entrance suggests an Art Deco inflection—the style's interest in mathematics and geometry being an appropriate choice for this building—as three fixed-light steel windows beneath a massive limestone frieze create the linear symmetry associated with this aesthetic.

Hasbrouck has the unique feature of a series of circular classrooms facing toward the Campus Pond. The addition by Desmond and Lord is strikingly, proudly modern, with its brushed steel columns, utterly flat facade, and rooftop line of windows.

The semicircular tower on the west elevation of the 1950 Hasbrouck Laboratory holds classrooms.

26. Integrated Sciences Building
Payette Associates, 2009

New Laboratory Science Building
Wilson Architects, 2013

The UMass campus has on the order of 2.8 million gross square feet of space. Yet two relatively recent buildings are designed to dramatically increase the amount of laboratory teaching and research space and provide updated facilities for a new generation of students and researchers.

The Integrated Sciences Building, a hulking new neighbor to Hasbrouck, Skinner, and East Experiment Station, is one of the largest new buildings on campus. With 157,000 square feet, the ISB is the anchor to a new complex rising in phases to the east and up the hill, creating a new quad for laboratory sciences.

Payette Associates used a site once occupied by the Marshall Hall and Marshall Annex (bacteriological research buildings; the annex was originally barracks moved from Westover Air Force base in Chicopee in 1947) that had come to be used by studio arts students until both were torn down in anticipation of the ISB. Payette is well known in the area, having designed Amherst College's Beneski Earth Sciences Building & Museum of Natural History (2006), not to mention dozens of science buildings on university campuses around the country. The building boasts 85,000 square feet of modern classrooms and laboratories, and a 300-seat auditorium, research labs, and faculty offices. It is designed around a new approach to science, which is to provide teaching and research spaces that bring together chemical, physical, and life sciences. The mission is made manifest with a four-story atrium that visually links the floors; a stairway bridges the space, twenty feet up. The atrium is named in honor of three Mahoney brothers—William (Class of 1954), Richard (Class of 1955), and Robert (Class of 1970)—each of whom graduated with chemistry degrees from UMass and went on to great success.

Built amidst a growing concern about energy consumption, the ISB was constructed with a number of "green" elements, including systems that harness rainwater from the roofs to cool air conditioning equipment, and extensive roof gardens. Early in the new century the University committed to making all new buildings at least meet LEED Silver certification for energy efficiency. The building won several awards from the Boston Society of Architects in 2010 and 2011.

Adjacent to the ISB and framing a new science quadrangle is the New Laboratory Science Building, designed by Wilson Architects. The building follows the ISB's lead in providing laboratory space for interdisciplinary research, but makes it even more flexible to accommodate as-yet-unknown directions for scientific research. The building curves along the slope of Prexy's Ridge, offering views to the woods and to the mountains to the west. A rooftop greenhouse is planned for the future.

Integrated Sciences Building

27. Worcester Dining Commons
Maloney and Tessier, 1953

From 1903 to the mid-twentieth century, the only dining hall on campus was in Draper Hall. It was designed to serve a student body of about 300, but by the late 1940s it was serving ten times that number. In 1948 the Van Meter building program responded to the strain by proposing to double student capacity on the 700-acre campus within three years. Worcester Dining Hall was an early part of that program, and was only the second freestanding dining commons on campus (student dining facilities were operated in both Greenough and Butterfield dormitories while Draper served as the main dining facility for the rest of the community). Like Hasbrouck Laboratory, still new when ground was broken for the dining commons, the building arranged rectangles of brick and glass to produce a modern effect beneath traditional cladding of brick. A two-story entrance of square windows is framed by thin columns, giving a classical tone to this postwar building. Both Louis Warren Ross's 1957 Student Union and James H. Ritchie's 1959 Morrill Building would borrow the square glazing motif. Springfield architects Morris W. Maloney (architect of Boyden Gym and part of the Merrill Science Center) and Henry J. Tessier focused their attention on the northern entrance, which gestures to an axis between the Northeast residential dormitories. It is one of the many after-the-fact axes created at UMass that have developed over so many years.

Worcester Dining Hall, its 69,000-square-foot dining facility, was quickly deemed insufficient and an addition to the dining hall was constructed in 1961.

The Worcester Dining Commons upon construction

West Experiment Station

28. West Experiment Station
Emory A. Ellsworth, 1887

This picturesque brick building, built in the 1880s, was the home of the State Agricultural Experiment Station, the first experiment station on a state college campus in the United States. By 1878 William Clark, Levi Stockbridge, and Charles Goessmann had already launched studies of crops, fruits, fertilizers, and other subjects, and in 1882, the Commonwealth began funding agricultural investigation. By 1885 planning had begun for this facility, made a reality in 1887, after the Hatch Act allowed federal funds to support state agricultural experiment stations. When a second station was built just across the street to the east, this building became known as the Hatch and later the West Experiment Station.

Hatch Experiment Station Laboratory.

West Experiment Station

Of the four surviving designs on campus offered by Holyoke, Massachusetts, architect Emory Alexander Ellsworth, this—his earliest—is arguably the most successful. Barre native Ellsworth was a member of the so-called Pioneer Class who entered in 1867; he served as president of the Alumni Association in 1877. His plans for this innovative enterprise called for a polychromatic brick building in the Queen Anne style, its porte cochere, rounded corner under a conical roof, and narrow windows beneath segmental arches all being hallmarks of the era. The heavy stone columns topped with leafy capitals complement the contrasting surfaces so popular in the Victorian era: gray stone bases, heavy brownstone, and red brick are enlivened by patterned brickwork as well as several Tudor Revival chimney stacks. The ground floor housed offices of the station's director and assistants, as well as two labs; upstairs were bedrooms as well as one of the several museums that have dotted the campus.

Today, a stone just east of the building under a red maple marks the onetime end of Ellis Drive (a companion marker sits near the bus stop next to the Fine Arts Center), and the rows of American elms that once lined it from the Experiment Station to the ravine west of the campus center garage.

29. East Experiment Station

Emory A. Ellsworth, 1890

In 1885 Emory A. Ellsworth was hired to draw plans for another building dedicated to agricultural research, and two years later, again with funds from the Hatch Act, construction began.

Built on the heels of the West Experiment Station, the building is one of the few extant examples on campus of Richardson Romanesque style (another being the Old Chapel). The style, and this building, are defined by the broad round arches, heavy stone construction, and dark and deep openings and windows. Stained glass windows—a feature found almost nowhere else on campus—also enliven the exterior.

Originally intended to house facilities for experimentation in agriculture, horticulture, entomology, and meteorology (with projects related to chemistry remaining in the West Experiment Station), the building contained, among other things, a fully equipped photographic studio with an overhead rail system for transporting large plant specimens to cameras. In the 1890s, the Station had an attached shed, glass house, and ornate Victorian greenhouse that were later removed.

The building now serves as the home of the University of Massachusetts Press. Founded in 1963 during the tenure of John W. Lederle, the University of Massachusetts Press publishes books in the humanities and social sciences, and especially in American Studies, as well as works for a general readership. Notable series include Native Americans of the Northeast, Culture and Politics in the Cold War, and Public History in Historical Perspective.

East Experiment Station, with greenhouse in the rear

30. Northeast Residential Area
Louis Warren Ross, 1959

While the student population in the early twentieth century had continued to rise, creating demand for additional and improved campus facilities in the 1920s and 1930s, with the onset of the Great Depression, prospects for added investment in the campus seemed bleak. By late 1933, however, the economic stimulus initiatives of the Federal Government meant that National Recovery Act funds were now available for the construction of a library, a new administration building, and other needed buildings. Among other things, the Massachusetts State College needed more housing for students. Even during the Great Depression, the student body had grown more than 40 percent, to 1,220 students. The only campus dorm for women, the Abigail Adams House, was completely filled. As a result, the administration stopped admitting women students in 1932.

From this pent-up demand emerged one of the largest building projects of the young Massachusetts State College. This dormitory complex at the southeast corner of North Pleasant Street and Eastman Lane—the Northeast Residential Area, comprising ten neo-Georgian structures built between 1935 and 1959—are laid out in a bilaterally symmetrical plan surrounding an open grassed area known as the Quad.

This elegant complex, whose rigorous symmetry is only visible once you leave North Pleasant Street and enter the courtyard, was UMass's version of the massive residential dormitory construction projects at Harvard, Yale, and other old private universities. Indeed, the Georgian details of Lewis House (1940), at the top of the Quad, are similar to those at Harvard's Dunster House (1930). Perhaps most striking is that even as the campus embraced modern design—hesitantly but still noticeably with buildings like the Student Union and Hasbrouck Hall—it remained committed over a quarter century (from 1935 to 1959) to the neo-Georgian style, as it struggled to complete this unified residential quad. Boston architect Louis Warren Ross's first building at UMass was Thatcher House in 1935, on the southeast corner of the Quad site. It is the most elaborately ornamented and rigorously detailed of Ross' Georgian reproductions, with corner quoins, complicated brickwork and keystones, and faux balustrades. (In a sly acknowledgment of the always-shifting funding from the state, Ross built the dormitories on the four corners of the site first, in order to establish this as space for a dormitory complex and nothing else.)

The Northeast Residential Area was redesignated a women's complex in 1947, its development guided by Helen Curtis Cole, dean of women from 1945 to 1973. In 1945 three dorms—Butterfield, Lewis and Thatcher—housed 410 women (with another 200-plus female students housed by the half-dozen sororities and area boarding houses). The new dean's top priority at the conclusion of her first year was improving the residential life of the students in her charge. Not long thereafter, construction of new dorm facilities commenced with L-shaped structures to define the constellation's boundaries; Hamilton and Knowlton rose in 1949 at the west, with Crabtree and Leach balancing at the east in 1953. The following year the district's North Pleasant street

This aerial view shows the symmetric arrangement around the quad; it is hard to imagine today another dorm being tucked inside this open courtyard, as planners once contemplated. Note the small white house in the center field, the 1731 Homestead, before its move to Stodbridge Road (see Walk Three).

boundary was completed with the construction of Arnold Hall (named in honor of Sarah Louise Arnold. the first dean at Boston's Simmons College and the first female trustee of Massachusetts Agricultural College), a long rectangular structure with low flanking blocks connected to Knowlton and Hamlin via breezeways and united visually by the cupola atop Arnold.

The dean ensured that the design of these buildings reflected her priorities, including social spaces where women could appropriately entertain male callers. The new dorms also included residential apartments for house mothers, who embodied the policies summarized as *in loco parentis* (that is, in the place of a parent) that aimed to govern student behavior. Closing hours, prohibitions concerning male visitors, and other rules sought to assure parents that the rising numbers of young women on campus would be well protected and well monitored.

While most of the buildings in the complex are named in honor of accomplished academic women who made contributions to the life of the campus, Crabtree House (1953) is more whimsically named for Charlotte "Lotta" Mignon Crabtree (1847–1924), a child star during the California Gold Rush who went on to become a vaudevillian once known as the "Nation's Darling." In the 1880s, during the same years that many buildings rose, Crabtree was among America's highest-paid performers. In her later years Crabtree became an activist on behalf of both women's suffrage and animal rights. She retired to Massachusetts and in her will established eight private charitable trusts in Boston that supported a number of constituencies, from disabled veterans of World War I to former convicts. The largest, an agricultural trust fund, today supports fellowships for UMass students in agricultural and natural resource majors. Some speculate today that it was a romantic attachment to someone at MAC that led to the gift.

The buildings continue to serve as dormitories (except for Arnold House, converted into offices in 1966); Thatcher House (1935), today the oldest extant dorm on campus, is a residence hall dedicated to languages; Chinese, French, German, Italian, Japanese, and Spanish each occupy a floor, which includes its own classroom.

31. Sylvan Residential Area
John Carl Warnecke and Associates, 1971

Situated in a slightly more remote site than other housing complexes on campus, the Sylvan Residential Area is surrounded by forest. One might suppose that the name of the complex refers to its woodland setting on the edge of campus, but in fact it honors Harry E. Sylvan, a university trustee from 1940 to 1968. The individual buildings are also named for former trustees: William M. Cashin, Harry Dunlap Brown, and Elizabeth L. McNamara. These nine-story brick buildings house 1,400 students.

Designed by celebrated architect John Carl Warnecke, the Sylvan dormitory opened in 1971 and was one of the first in the country to use a suite-style layout. The suites each contain one bathroom, a common living area, and a combination of double and single rooms that house anywhere from six to eight students. This arrangement

Sylvan Residential Area upon construction

was originally intended for engineering students to live in a common space where they could collaborate on their studies. Today, the dorm houses students in all areas of study.

Warnecke's other projects included dorms for both Stanford University and the University of California, Berkeley; the Oakland, California, airport (1962); and several buildings at the Naval Academy in Annapolis (1965). Perhaps most notably, Warnecke grew close to the Kennedys following his involvement in historic preservation efforts to save historic townhouses in Lafayette Square in Washington, D.C., from demolition. President Kennedy nominated him to the Fine Arts Commission, and after the president's assassination, Jacqueline Kennedy requested that he design the president's gravesite at Arlington National Cemetery, with its iconic eternal flame.

32. North Area Residence Apartments
Architectural Resources Cambridge, 2006

The pressures of expansion and demand from the town that UMass accommodate more students on campus (and fewer in residential neighborhoods) led to the first major dorm expansion in forty years (when Sylvan, just to the east, was built), with the completion of North Residence Apartments in 2006. Following the trend in dormitory design and with an eye toward recruiting more out-of-state students, North is composed of apartment-style dorms, with full kitchens in a suite arrangement. Each five-story building houses approximately 200 students, for a total of 850. Overall, UMass has on-campus living spaces for more than 14,000 students. The four L-shaped buildings create two intimate quadrangles that aim to foster a sense of community among these residents while also encouraging friendly competition among the houses.

When drafting plans for the Harold Alfond Management Center, Architectural Resources Cambridge emphasized modern materials and lines, but in the design of these residence halls, they took a more traditional approach in buildings that harness popular historical imagery surrounding New England college architecture. In fact, the deep red brickwork and steeply pitched gables and rooflines resonate with South College and seem almost to make conscious allusion to Brocklesby's Victorian cottages on the campus of nearby Smith College.

North Area Residence Apartments

33. Ruth J. Totman Gymnasium
Thomas Mott Shaw for Perry, Shaw, Hepburn, Kehoe & Dean, 1959

During the period of rapid growth following the World War II, Machmer Hall and the Student Union were both under construction in the heart of campus while Totman Gymnasium rose on the northeast edge. Built to house the Department of Physical Education for Women, affectionately known as WoPE, the facility was renamed in 1984 to honor Ruth Jane Totman (1894–1989), a professor and head of the department from 1943 to '64.

Born in 1894, Ruth Totman graduated from Sargent College of Physical Education in 1916 and taught elementary and secondary school physical education in New York and Pennsylvania for a number of years. She also received a BS from Douglas College, then known as the New Jersey College for Women. She completed an MA in education from the University of Pittsburgh in 1934.

In 1943 she was invited to head the Department of Physical Education for Women at Massachusetts State. With large numbers of men enrolled serving in the war, the presence of women on campus was much larger. After the campus became the University of Massachusetts in 1946, Totman continued to grow her program to match the mounting enrollments. After the construction of the Curry S. Hicks Physical Education Building for Men in 1931, physical education classes for women were moved to the newly renovated Drill Hall, which was shared with ROTC.

In 1943 Totman became the director of the Department of Physical Education for Women. She expanded the course offerings and hired two new staff members to compensate for a growing female population. Young women were required to take physical education classes each year, with classes three times a week for freshmen and sophomores and class twice a week for juniors and seniors. Freshmen and sophomores were required to take one term of dance and play one team sport, while juniors and seniors took electives like archery, swimming, badminton, and golf. Required classes for juniors and seniors lasted until 1947. In 1953 the department added courses in educating elementary and secondary students in physical education.

In 1956 the Drill Hall, then the home of women's physical education, was destroyed by an electrical fire, presenting both a crisis and an opportunity. Totman devoted the next year to designing a new gym. The cornerstone for the new women's gym was laid on November 2, 1957. The building was designed by Perry, Shaw, Hepburn, Kehoe & Dean of Boston and was constructed by M. J. Walsh & Sons of Holyoke. The new gym boasted a swimming pool, two basketball courts, six bowling lanes, and an indoor archery range, in addition to much-needed office space.

Founded in 1923, the Boston firm Perry, Shaw & Hepburn is more often remembered today as the architects responsible for the restoration of Colonial Williamsburg in the 1920s and 30s (as well as "The Coop," a neo-Georgian Harvard University landmark). In 1950 the firm had designed Kendall Hall, another gymnasium, for Mount Holyoke College. For the physical education building at UMass, the firm offered a modern design that would resonate well with Hasbrouck Hall and the Worcester Dining

Ruth J. Totman Gymnasium

Hall, which sits to the south. The building fronts on Eastman Lane (called "Lover's Lane" in the 1930s and '40s) rather than North Pleasant Street. The green glass blocks mark the basketball courts at the heart of the building. Circular windows echo the Student Union's design of the previous year and even allude to the nearby neo-Georgian Johnson Hall, one of the most elaborate of neo-Georgian buildings on the campus. The entrance has the reserved, but elegant, fee of a 1950s post office, with concrete fluted pilasters with the most subtle of details. Inside is a cavernous glazed-brick lobby, with arched staircases leading to the upper floors.

In 1958 "WoPE," the new Women's Physical Education Building, opened and was considered one of the largest and finest women's physical education buildings in the nation. The same year a major in physical education for women was available for the first time. The courses emphasized preparation for teaching in elementary and secondary schools as well as instructing sports and dance for camps and civic centers.

The building was renamed for Totman in 1984 after years of lobbying from alumni, faculty, staff, and administration members. Naming the building for Totman while she still lived required an exception to University policy, which only permitted memorializing individuals in the naming of buildings after their death. Warren McGuirk, dean of the School of Physical Education, was one of the most vocal advocates of naming the gym for Totman and lobbied the chancellor and trustees for the change. The trustees finally voted to change the name on June 6, 1984. Above the interior lobby, Totman looks down from a portrait, approvingly, at athletes and visitors entering her gym.

34. Institute for Holocaust, Genocide, and Memory Studies
ca. 1928; addition, Ray Kinoshita Mann, 2005

In the nineteenth century, the land on which this house now stands was part of the extensive holdings of the Cowles family, whose lumber operation anchored the community of North Amherst for over two centuries. In 1895 James and Nancy Cowles transferred the land on which this house stands to their son Arthur F. Cowles, who in turn sold it to Professor of Agriculture William Penn Brooks (1851–1938). Brooks had been a member of MAC's Class of 1875; he returned to MAC to pursue graduate work in chemistry and botany, and in 1877 joined William Smith Clark in Japan. He would remain at Sapporo Agricultural School for twelve years, serving for four years as that college's president. In 1889, Brooks returned to MAC as a professor of agriculture; he also began to serve as an engineer at the Massachusetts Agricultural Experiment Station. During this time, among other things, Brooks introduced soybeans to the United States. He served as president of MAC from 1905 until 1906. Today, Brooks House in the Central Residence Area is named for him.

In 1928 Brooks developed the land around this house, conveying one lot to Bill Gass (1902–1986), a local contractor whose hand shaped much of the housing stock in the Pioneer Valley, and it seems likely that he designed this house as well. Perhaps best known for his work assisting Henry and Helen Flynt with their restoration of nearby Historic Deerfield, Gass attended Deerfield Academy before going to work for his father, also a building contractor. The modest Tudor Revival dwelling joined a neighborhood of Colonial and Tudor Revival houses that borders campus to the North.

Institute for Holocaust, Genocide, and Memory Studies

The Institute's exhibition space

In 1972 the house was sold to the Diocese of Western Massachusetts of the Protestant Episcopal Church and became the Five College Episcopal Center, a minis-try of the Diocese of Western Massachusetts. As a result, tucked inside this structure is one of the gems that makes up the campus's architectural legacy. In 2003, Five College Episcopal minister Chris Carlisle asked UMass architecture professor Ray Kinoshita Mann to do the impossible: take the existing garage—shape, structure, and all—and turn it into a sacred space suitable for prayer services adjacent to the min-istry offices as well as meetings, exhibits, and gatherings for guest speakers. Mann used every inch of the erstwhile garage to carve out a warm room where light streams in from windows sliced out of the roof as well as the rear garden (itself designed by UMass landscape architecture professor Dean Cardasis, creator of the garden by Durfee greenhouses). Dubbed "the Ark," short for the Ark Episcopal Chaplaincy, the minimalist space opened in 2005 and served its intended purposes until the ministry chose to relocate.

In 2010 the building became home to the Institute for Holocaust, Genocide, and Memory Studies. Professor James E. Young, an internationally renowned scholar of Holocaust and memory studies and a leading authority worldwide on memorial and commemorative art, founded the Institute. The facility is home to a perma-nent Holocaust teaching exhibition, A Reason to Remember, formerly housed in the Hatikvah Holocaust Education Center in Springfield, Massachusetts, and generously donated to the University by the Jewish Federation of Western Massachusetts in November 2010.

Orchard Hill

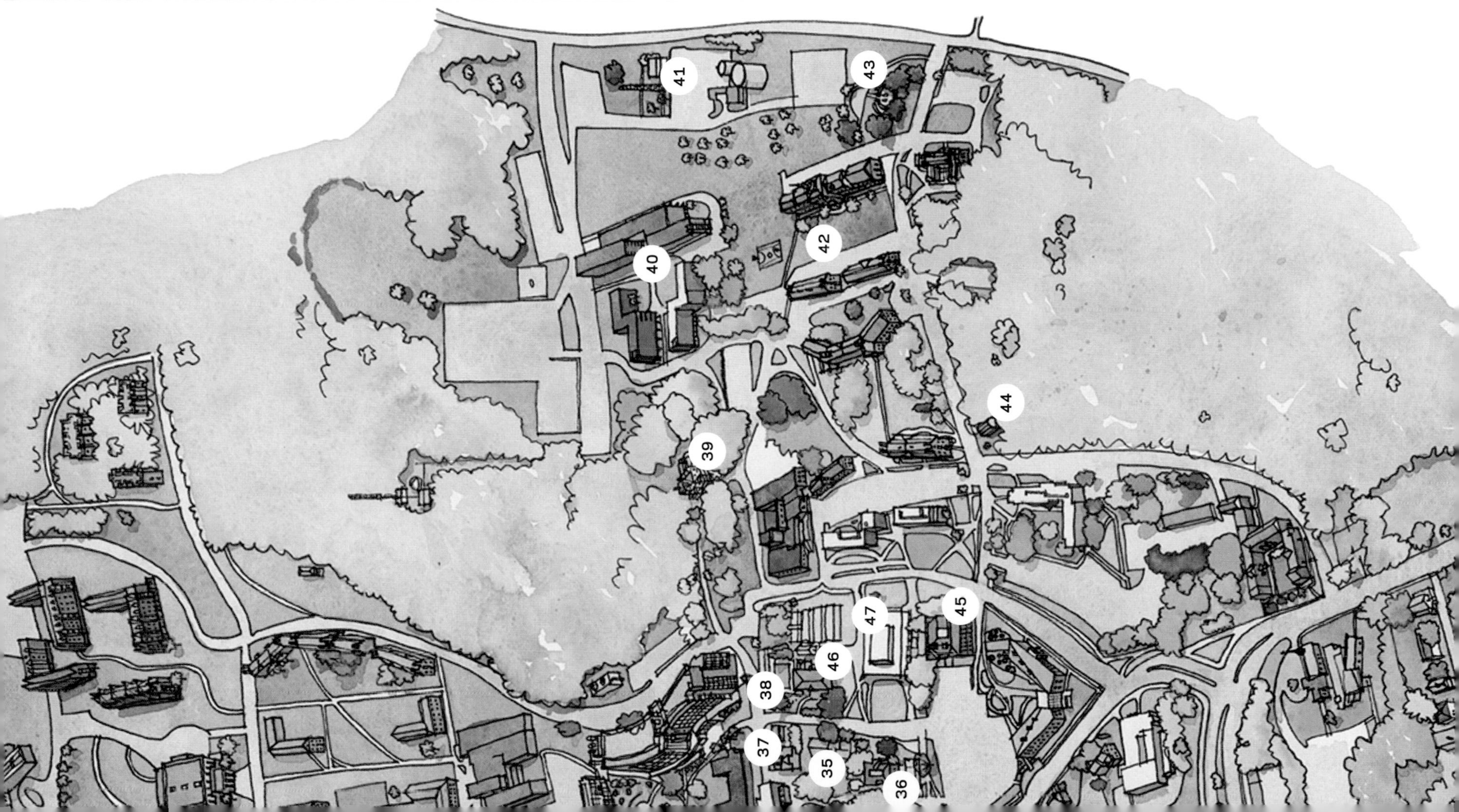
35
36
37
38
39
40
41
42
43
44
45
46
47

Walk Three: Orchard Hill

Orchard Hill is named for the stand of apple trees that once occupied the wooded rise that forms the eastern horizon of the modern campus. The nineteenth-century "Clark's orchard" refers to William Smith Clark, well known for bringing back plant specimens from his trips to Japan; in and around the apple orchards grew cherry and plum trees, as well as raspberries, blackberries, and strawberries. Market garden plots filled in land between French Hall and Butterfield Terrace, and the campus even made an attempt at a vineyard.

In time, the orchards were removed to provide dormitory space at the rapidly expanding University, and the pomology program relocated to Belchertown at the former Hanifin Farm. Donated to the University by the Massachusetts Fruit Growers' Association in 1962, the farm was renamed Cold Spring Orchard in honor of the original name of the community just east of Amherst, rechristened Belchertown (in honor of Jonathan Belcher, governor of the colony of Massachusetts from 1730 to 1741) when it was incorporated in 1761.

Alongside the orchards stood the twenty-four-acre Prexy's Ridge Forest ("prexy" being a shorthand reference to the university president, whose home, Hillside, stands here), woods that filled the steep westward slope of this glacial drumlin. Unsuitable for agriculture, this land and its vegetation had been drawn upon by the region's indigenous peoples before European settlement; today a rare old-growth forest, these woods have served as a site of forestry education for over a century and a half.

Today the former orchards and contemporary woodlands are encompassed within the University's Waugh Arboretum. Interest in a campus arboretum

This March 1953 view of Fernald Hall and the onetime "insectary" captures Stockbridge Road's evolution.

The construction of Greenough Hall

blossomed (so to speak) under the leadership of Frank A. Waugh (1869–1943), head of the landscape architecture department in the early twentieth century. Waugh is best remembered today for his work promoting recreation in our national forests; he took a highly natural approach to landscape design, and endorsed choices grounded in ecology. He was also among the first landscape architects to articulate a distinct American landscape architecture tradition. At UMass, Waugh envisioned a picturesque campus where buildings blend with the agricultural landscape, a point of view that accurately reflected the founding principle of the college: the land was more important than the buildings.[1] After Waugh's death in 1944, Massachusetts State College President Hugh Baker recommended that certain areas of campus be set aside for creation of the Waugh Arboretum, to be overseen by the Department of Landscape Architecture.

The arboretum "slipped from the university's consciousness in the 1960s," the *Boston Globe* noted in 2001, when the "great building boom on campus saw trees as obstacles rather than assets," but today the arboretum—redefined to encompass the whole campus—boasts 1,500 species across 1,400 acres.[2] Orchard Hill retains mature forests on its summit and western slope. Specimen trees scattered across campus include grand beech, sweet gum, and tulip trees.

This walk begins along Stockbridge Road, named for Levi Stockbridge, the fifth president of the college. The path that came to bear his name was laid out sometime in the first quarter of the eighteenth century, an alternative to "West Street" (now East Pleasant Street), which ran along the ridge. Sometime before 1728, Hadley families eager to settle on the flatter land of the ridge's eastern slope in what was still, until 1759, Hadley's "east precinct" developed this more practical route to Sunderland. The earliest printed map of Amherst, published in 1833 (created by Charles Baker Adams and Alonzo Gray of the Amherst College Class of

Central Residential Area

1834), shows Stockbridge Road as it leaves town center, passing by several Cowles residences before heading on to the "North Parish," today's North Amherst.

The historic buildings along this road developed in phases. For more than a century, farmhouses like the Boltwood-Stockbridge House (named for Stockbridge, who lived here in the years he helped establish the new campus) were the principal buildings along the road, set within constellations of farms and outbuildings. This era was followed in the 1860s by the first buildings of MAC, the Durfee Plant House (1867) being the oldest. Another phase of development stretched from 1906 to '09 and included the building of Wilder Hall, Clark Hall, Clark Hall Greenhouse, French Hall Greenhouse, and French Hall. In 1955 the "Durfee Range" was added to replace the original Durfee Plant House, which had burned down. Stockbridge in these years was a tree-lined way on a scale conducive to the integration of residential-style houses with small academic buildings.

North Pleasant Street, laid out in 1866, increasingly trumped Stockbridge Road as the principal northward path through campus. Despite the appearance of French and Fernald Halls and the Franklin Dining Commons, Stockbridge Road gradually lost its function as a road linking Sunderland and Amherst and became a service road for the campus. The recent construction of the Studio Arts Building at the south end and the Integrated Science Buildings at the north has turned the old road into "little more than a very wide sidewalk." [3]

An especially vigorous phase of development on the eastern edge of the University came with the mid-twentieth-century construction of residence areas on this hillside. By the 1960s and '70s, the dormitories in this section of campus became important sites of student activism and in time the home of some of the important campus organizations to emerge from those tempestuous years.

35. University Club
1728 and 1731

The University Club sits within two structures that date from the era of the Great
Awakening: the Boltwood-Stockbridge House (1728) and the Cowles Homestead,
both built around 1730 in what were then the eastern fringes of Hadley. Both are good
examples of the classic New England saltbox, reflecting the architectural preferences
of second- and third-generation English settlers. Framed houses had appeared in
the Connecticut Valley with the first English migrants, but the first wave of housing
produced small, one-over-one houses without much ornamentation. By the second
quarter of the eighteenth century, the Valley towns had seen dramatic change: the
threat of attacks on English settlements had been greatly reduced, and in an atmosphere of comparative security and stability, trade flourished and prosperity rose.
The hall-and-parlor plan, centered around the massive center chimney, became a
mark of that prosperity.

The Boltwood-Stockbridge House was originally built by Samuel and Hannah
Boltwood. A number of families had gathered in Hadley's "east precinct"—enough that
by the early 1730s the eighteen or so residents had established their own church and
burying ground. In 1759 the community was set off from Hadley and named Amherst
in honor of the forty-two-year-old Lord Jeffrey Amherst, a military hero in the war
with France who had just enjoyed a spectacular victory in the capture of the fort
at Louisburg, on the northeast coast of Nova Scotia. Two decades later, during the
American Revolution, the Amherst Committee on Safety confined nine local men sus-
pected of being "unfriendly to their country" to this house, which then was the home of
Lieutenant John Field.

The building that now stands next door, known as "The Homestead," was built
in 1731 by John Cowles on the site of what is now the Lederle Graduate Research
Center. It is distinguished from the Boltwood-Stockbridge House in part by the framed

The University Club courtyard

Stockbridge House

*"The Homestead" once served as a practice facility
for students in Home Economics*

overhang of the second floor, an embellishment derived from a building type associated with early seventeenth-century English cities.

Both houses were purchased about 1864 with the land that became the Massachusetts Agricultural College. The Boltwood-Stockbridge House became the home of Henry Flagg French, the first president of MAC—making it also then the boyhood home of Daniel Chester French, the sculptor who would go on to create the memorial to the minuteman installed at Concord, Massachusetts (1875), and the statue of Abraham Lincoln seated in the Lincoln Memorial in Washington, D.C. (1920). After Flagg resigned in 1867, Levi Stockbridge made the house his residence and office.

The Cowles house had served as the residence for the farmer in charge of the Massachusetts State Agricultural Experiment Station until 1929, when the building was renovated to become a so-called Practice House for the College's flourishing home economics program. Female students lived together here, under the guidance of a resident faculty member, in conditions intended to simulate the realities of family life on a moderate income.

In 1934, the Boltwood-Stockbridge House became the home of the MAC faculty club, open only to members. Segregated lounge spaces entertained (male) faculty and their wives; the latter had access to the house for afternoon parties and occasional evenings (and in 1948, in something of an odd juxtaposition, the Shade Tree Laboratory was established in the southwestern section of the building, where the carriage shed and stable wing had once been located). By the 1960s, the University's growing faculty had begun to overwhelm the space. In 1967, as plans progressed to build a large research facility on the site of the onetime Cowles farm, a proposal

The University Club dining room

emerged to move the Cowles house to the site of the club, adjoining Stockbridge House, thus doubling the size of the facility. In 1972, the two dwellings were joined by a passageway.

Since 2008, the University Club & Restaurant has been open to the public and serves seasonal, contemporary New England cuisine in this historic setting.

Clark Hall, circa 1919

36. Clark Hall
Frank Irving Cooper of Cooper and Bailey, 1907

Clark Hall was named for William Smith Clark (1826–1886), third president of the Massachusetts Agricultural College (1867–79) and professor of botany. The onetime home of the Department of Botany, the building holds two sizeable lecture halls, a seminar room, and labs for undergraduate and graduate students. The attic originally housed faculty quarters; occupants looking west took in majestic views of the Valley. Morrill Science Center, whose southern end stands outside Clark Hall's western entrance, gave Botany modern new spaces. For many years, Clark Hall was used as painting studios by the Department of Art. Plans are afoot for new uses for this building, including the possibility that it may provide a new home for the University Museum of Contemporary Art, housed in the Fine Arts Center since 1974.

The building's style is sometimes considered a late representation of the American Round Arch Style (otherwise known as *Rundbogenstil*) combining Romanesque and Renaissance elements, usually identified with buildings from the mid-nineteenth century. The eclectic blend of Georgian Revival, Renaissance Revival, and Romanesque seem suited to its current site. Clark jostles up against Colonial Stockbridge and Modernist Morrill and Franklin, and stands across from contemporaneous neo-Georgian

French. The building is distinguished by its full-height arched windows and heavy dentils under the eaves. To appreciate the design, one must remember that the grand entrances were designed to frame sweeping views from both east and west—to the orchards of Clark Hill to the east, and across the fields to the Holyoke Range to the southwest.

Interior of Clark Hall, circa 1919

37. Wilder Hall
Walter R. B. Willcox, 1905

A picturesque, cinnamon-colored brick building with brown terra-cotta trim, Wilder Hall was originally designed for the study of market gardening, floriculture, greenhouse management, and landscape gardening. In fact, it was the first building in the United States designed specifically to house a landscape architecture program.

Planned under the leadership of MAC President Goodell, Wilder Hall was one of several research and instructional buildings that aimed to improve the College's facilities at the turn of the twentieth century. Walter R. B. Willcox's design was influenced by Frank Lloyd Wright and the Prairie Style (though it predates by thirty-five years the lone example of Wright's work in Amherst, the 1940 Baird House at 38 Shays Street) and is considered one of the University's gems. Willcox was based in Burlington, Vermont, and most of his work was in that state. In 1907 he moved to Seattle and then to Eugene, Oregon, where he became the chair of the School of Architecture at the University of Oregon.

Willcox created a distinctive building by mixing elements of the Mission Revival and Arts and Crafts styles. The green tile roof and broad overhangs are reminiscent of Mission buildings, while the exposed rafters, sloping terra-cotta brackets and low-pitched hip roofs suggest Arts and Crafts influences. A lovely balcony on the first floor faces west, with terra-cotta framed arched openings (now covered) that originally offered views into the Reading Room. A nameplate above the recessed doorway dedicates the building to Marshall P. Wilder, whose mid-nineteenth-century advocacy on behalf of agricultural education is often acknowledged as central to MAC's origins.

Wilder Hall

The Durfee Conservatory today and Durfee Gardens

38. Durfee Conservatory
T. A. Lord, 1867; Lord & Burnham, 1954

The original Durfee Conservatory—a series of glass buildings held together with wrought-iron filigree and covered with curved roofs—was one of the most striking structures on what was the fairly barren landscape of the young college. Built just before the arrival of the first students, it quickly became a symbol of the new college and its possibilities. Rebuilt after a fire in 1883, the conservatory slowly declined and was taken down and reconstructed in 1954 by the original firm, Lord & Burnham. The latter iteration was much improved: one of the first aluminum-alloy frame conservatories to be built in the United States, it boasted automatic temperature and air controls. At the turn of the twenty-first century, the lone hint of the original building is the single-curved glass pane along the eaves and the double-door entrance in the central range. But for all its technological advances, the new building is far more utilitarian than the original Victorian structure.

Durfee Gardens, surrounding the Conservatory, was designed by Dean Cardasis, longtime professor of Landscape Architecture. Cardasis sought to reclaim an order to an agricultural landscape—the orchards, fields, and vineyards that once covered this hillside—which had been rendered

The original Durfee Conservatory

A glimpse of Durfee Gardens

chaotic by a series of unplanned changes over time. Using the clarity of a grid, he designed a series of contemporary garden spaces that nonetheless borrow from the historical uses and plantings of the region. Stones from the Berkshire Hills and round stones from the Connecticut River Valley make a path alongside existing beech and spruce trees, as well as new plantings of birch and mountain laurel. A square of grass creates an island of repose, made more lively by eleven eighteen-foot-tall translucent trellises. Cardasis won several prestigious landscape architecture awards for Durfee Gardens, including an honor award from the American Society of Landscape Architects, the highest award given for landscape design.

39. Hillside, The Chancellor's House
Unknown, 1885

Hillside, constructed in 1885 to serve as the home of the college president, was sited at the south end of Prexy's Ridge. Paul Chadbourne selected the location, which overlooked the horticulture department. The home—unlike that of many campus leaders elsewhere—does not attempt to make a public statement, but rather is secluded and out of the way. Both the second and sixth president of the college, Chadbourne left Massachusetts to serve as president and professor of metaphysics at another new land-grant institution, the University of Wisconsin–Madison, but returned to Massachusetts in 1872 to lead Williams College. In 1882, he returned to accept a second term as president of the Massachusetts Agricultural College, his sights now set on financial aid, campus expansion, and curricular reform aimed at closing the gap between the agricultural college and the more established liberal arts colleges. Chadbourne stipulated that the construction of a dedicated residence for the college president would be a condition of his return. Construction was delayed when the funds ran out; another allocation—to complete Hillside House and to commence work on what would become the Old Chapel—was made, but too late for Chadbourne, who died in 1883.

For the home of the leader of the campus, Hillside has surprisingly obscure origins. No architect is identified with the house, which was probably constructed by a local builder. Like the rest of campus, the building evolved over time, with changes and additions made as needed and as budgets would allow. Early on, the original side porch was enclosed and incorporated into the living room, the front porch transformed into a sun room, and the back porch converted to the entrance. Aluminum siding was slapped over wooden clapboarding. But the outstanding features and the setting remain. As does the history: for more than a century the dwelling has housed presidents and chancellors of the University of Massachusetts and their families.

Hillside, home of the university chancellor

One long-term resident of Hillside was Kenyon Butterfield, who became president of MAC in 1906 and remained in that position until 1924, and who shared the home with his wife, Harriet. Although Butterfield was dedicated to his home field of rural sociology, he campaigned to broaden the curriculum of MAC, "to give instruction in the natural and social sciences so that it will yield that discipline and liberal training that belong to the educated man." [4]

Another resident, Ralph Van Meter, was the first of the new University of Massachusetts's presidents and it was under his tenure (1947–54) that the first wave of twenty post-war buildings were put up. When Ralph and Eudora Van Meter lived there, social events for the whole campus staff sustained the close connection between campus leadership and the employees. "I think there were about four hundred and fifty on the staff at that time," Eudora would later recall, "and by having several parties of one hundred and ten or so at a time, we could entertain the staff a couple of times a year." On Parents Day, the Van Meters threw a big lawn party. The campus provided no domestic help; the family engaged a housekeeper from nearby Cushman Village whom Mrs. Van Meter would pick up and take home each day. Three students also lived in the top floor and were expected to work around the house six hours each week, an hour each day, excluding Sunday. [5]

The most distinctive landscape feature of Hillside is the rhododendron garden, located just below the house. First planted in 1877, before Hillside was built, the garden includes many trees sent from Japan by President Clark. It became an even more prominent place with the construction of Hillside and was often the site of demonstrations by the horticultural department. Class commencements took place in the garden for many years. In 1940, the Stockbridge senior class donated stone entrance posts, which had belonged to the town of Prescott, but were removed before the town was flooded in 1938 to create the Quabbin Reservoir. In 1983, the garden was named in recognition of Professor Gordon S. King's thirty-two years of teaching in the Stockbridge School.

40. Orchard Hill Residential Area
Hugh Stubbins, 1957

Dickinson Hall, together with Grayson, Webster, and Field halls, all surrounding a central grassy area known as "The Bowl," comprise the Orchard Hill Residential Area. They were designed by Hugh Stubbins, architect of Franklin Dining Commons and the Southwest Residential Area complex.

Architectural Record in 1966 deemed Stubbins's Orchard Hill dorms "merely good" while Southwest boasted "brilliant, integrated design." [6] Stubbins, it was argued, was victim to the university's absence of clear vision. Because there was no master plan for the campus, much less for the dormitories intended for its eastern hillside, Stubbins had no way to know what architecture would surround his buildings or how they might be connected. In this absence he designed a symmetrical, inward-turning complex deficient of the drama of the Southwest buildings. What they lack in theatricality, however, they gain in setting. In spring and fall, the dormitories have some of the best views on campus.

It was the frustration of designing in the dark that led Stubbins to urge the university to hire a master planning firm to guide future development. On his recommendation, the university chose Sasaki, Walker & Associates in 1961 to update the 1957 master plan by Shurcliff, Shurcliff & Merrill.

Today, Orchard Hill is distinguished by offering "living and learning communities" for first-year students, with each dorm having a different social and intellectual emphasis: Science, Innovation, and Leadership in Dickinson Hall; Society and Leadership in Webster. Some floors are dedicated to Residential Academic Programs, experiences designed to help first-year students make a smooth transition to university life by engaging them in small communities that together study subjects of shared concern, from sustainability to social justice and activism to connections between science and society.

Orchard Hill Residential Area

41. Solar Habitat
Curtis Johnson, William Heronemus, and Duane E. Cromack, 1976

The Solar Habitat with the WF-1 *turbine*

Now falling into ruin, the small house behind the Orchard Hill Residential Area and in the shadow of the Town of Amherst's water towers is the Solar Habitat, a building of little architectural significance but great historical importance. One of the most advanced wind turbines of the era, a 25-kilowatt turbine known as WF-1 was installed here in the early 1970s and became the anchor of the University's Renewable Energy Research Laboratory (now the Wind Energy Center), helping establish the university's worldwide reputation as a leader in wind energy. WF-1 was paired with the Solar Habitat, which featured a number of sustainable building practices such as solar hot water. The habitat's design demonstrated how such technologies could be incorporated into the ranch-style houses popular at the time. The well-insulated six-room single-story building (funded by a Hatch Act grant) would be heated entirely by the wind turbine the largest working turbine in the United States and perhaps the largest in the world at the time of construction. The turbine was dismantled in 2004 and in 2010 entered the collections of the Smithsonian Institution.

42. Central Residential Area
Louis Warren Ross, 1940–1963

Clark Hill was steadily occupied by a neo-Georgian village in the middle of the last century, transforming the hillside of orchards and vineyards into a planned community for some of the thousands of new students rushing to take advantage of a UMass education.

Nine dorms rose over eighteen years, all designed by the prolific Louis Warren Ross. Like North Residential Area, also designed by Ross, Central is laid out in a Beaux-Arts plan with a central axis running north to south, perpendicular to the steep Clark Hill road, with the cupola atop Van Meter sitting at the center of the plan. The site was graded to allow for a series of terraces that serve as gathering spaces for students. The neo-Georgian style is most evident in the first buildings, at the top of the hill. As the last buildings rose, the vocabulary changed, becoming less overtly neo-Georgian. These buildings chart Ross's steady evolution on campus, culminating in the more overtly modernist Student Union in 1957.

The restrained demeanor of this cluster belies the dramatic relationship between these buildings and the student unrest of the late 1960s and early '70s.

Butterfield House, at the very top of the hill at the eastern edge of the campus, was completed in 1940, intended to house women on campus (the house was named for Kenyon Butterfield, who had been an advocate for women's program at MAC). Upon opening, it housed some 147 students. A ground-floor sitting room provided space to entertain male callers, and there was a small apartment designed to accommodate a house mother. Meals were prepared and served family style in a dedicated kitchen. It was Ross's first building for the campus and would set the neo-Georgian tone for the next two decades.

Butterfield's remote location, on the slope of Clark Hill and at a distance from campus (its closest neighbor at the time of construction being the small apiary below), its comparatively compact size, and the survival of that dedicated kitchen and dining facilities contributed to the distinct role the house came to play in campus life. The building was converted to a men's dorm early on, when female enrollment in the years immediately following the war plummeted, from 500 women in 1945 to 100 in '46. The Northeast cluster developed to serve women students, while Central saw additions (beginning with Chadbourne and Greenough halls) for men.

In time, Butterfield acquired a reputation as the home of "artists, musicians, vegetarians, draft counselors, and other independent spirits," as the building's small size and location on the edge of campus attracted students who saw themselves as outside the mainstream.[7] Importantly, as the 1940s gave way to the '50s and '60s, Butterfield retained its separate dining hall—which continued to serve meals family style, while other students used the grab-and-go dining halls emerging elsewhere on campus. The kitchen helped nurture the flowering of a distinct counterculture here, becoming a legendary corner of the campus community, as the 6:00 PM community meals created a sense of camaraderie in this house unlike anything elsewhere. As one student noted, "Serving each other bread, you become very close-knit. When you left UMass, you left with 150 best friends."[8]

Butterfield House

A signature pirate flag came to fly over the roof, symbolizing the community's independence. But a series of incidents inclined administrators to try to address some of the less desirable consequences of the Butterfield spirit; the hall's kitchen was closed in 2001 when the dorm was "reprogrammed" and the Butterfield community disbanded.

Greenough House opened six years after Butterfield, in 1946. Two decades later, the set of policies now dubbed *in loco parentis* had now governed student life—some would say strictly governed—for more than twenty years, while campus life had changed dramatically. By 1960, more than 2,000 women attended UMass, and soon student pressure would dismantle these policies. Coeducational dorms had appeared at the nearby University of Connecticut at Storrs by 1964, and as the women's movement and the sexual revolution unfolded across UMass, outdated policies were increasingly challenged. The curfew system was gradually curtailed. In summer 1969, students in Greenough House proposed that the hall be converted to a coed facility and in spring 1970, Greenough became the first dorm on campus to house women and men together, on alternate floors. By fall 1970, thirteen dorms on campus had gone coed, and by the following year, single-sex dorms were the exception rather than the rule. These years also witnessed the birth of three vital and enduring UMass Amherst entities for university women: the Everywoman's Center, the Women's Studies program, and the Status of Women Council.

Mills House (New Africa House) rose in 1948, the fourth in the series of nine. But today it no longer serves as a residential facility; instead, it houses the W. E. B. Du Bois Department of Afro-American Studies. In 1969, some of the first African-American students to attend UMass were housed in Mills, and the building quickly became a focus for conversations about race on campus. Today, a widespread misperception holds that "New Africa House" emerged as a result of a series of protests and occupations in 1970, but in truth, as early as the 1966–67 academic year, African American students and faculty, responding to the emergence nationwide of the field of Black Studies, had conceptualized a curriculum, cultural program, and supporting services at UMass. A formal proposal to establish this department was on the Faculty Senate agenda in March 1970 when tension between white and black students erupted into a full-blown takeover of the building, in which students demanded the creation of a black cultural center (the men then living in Mills, evicted during the occupation and necessarily relocated to Brooks House midsemester, de facto created the second coed dorm on campus). Whatever the degree to which the occupation influenced subsequent events, the department was established in 1970 and instantly became a leading center for the study of African American history and culture. A long-standing association with W. E. B. Du Bois and his family led to the department being named in his honor. Today, New Africa House is also home to the Augusta Savage Art Gallery (named for the influential sculptor), as well as the Everywoman's Center, one of the first women's centers in the nation, established in 1972.

Also in this constellation of dorms is Chadbourne House (1947), which today houses around 150 students as well as the Josephine White Eagle Native American Cultural Center. The sculptural tribute to Metawampe that dates from roughly the same period notwithstanding, there is a long tradition at UMass of serious study of Native American peoples and substantive engagement with living native tribes in New England. An expression of that commitment in Chadbourne House is the White Eagle Center, founded in 1989 and located here since 1991. Named for Dr. Josephine White Eagle, a faculty member in the School of Education and member of the Ho-Chunk Nation, the resource serves native students, staff, and faculty across the Five Colleges and raises cultural diversity awareness in the Pioneer Valley. In Thompson Hall, a Certificate Program in Native American Indian Studies (CPNAIS) "offers students a structured understanding of historical and contemporary issues affecting the Western Hemisphere's First Nations."[9] Fall pow-wows have also reminded the UMass community of the long history of indigenous people in the region.

43. William Smith Clark Memorial
Todd Richardson, 1991

The William Smith Clark Memorial stands atop a high ridge at the eastern edge of the campus, the onetime site of the gabled Victorian home of the Clark family. Born in 1826, Clark taught at Amherst College for fifteen years; in 1867 he became president of MAC. He championed education that was both well rounded and practical.

Horace Capron, the U.S. Commissioner of Agriculture, introduced Clark to a Japanese delegation visiting Washington, D.C. The Japanese government was in the process of annexing Hokkaido, its large northern island, and wanted to develop agriculture and associated industries on the island. In 1876 the government of Japan invited Clark and other MAC alumni to help found a similar college in Sapporo, Hokkaido.

William Smith Clark Memorial

Clark spent eight months as president of Sapporo Agriculture College (later Hokkaido Imperial University and today Hokkaido University) and was widely revered as the founder of modern agriculture in Japan. His farewell address, in which he called on his Japanese students to "be ambitious," became a slogan among students and is still repeated in Japanese school textbooks. The exchange between UMass and Hokkaido University continued over the next century, with students and faculty as well as trees and plants moving between the two institutions. The campus is dotted to this day with trees (such as the first Japanese elm in the United States, which still stands by South College) that Clark brought back or were brought as gifts in the ongoing friendship between the two institutions.

In the fall of 1986, Landscape Architecture and Regional Planning Professor Barrie B. Greenbie invited Asakawa Shoichiro from Hokkaido University's Department of Landscape Architecture and Takano Fumiaki, an alumnus of Hokkaido University and a practicing landscape architect, to direct an advanced design studio for graduate students at UMass. Students were invited to submit designs that referenced both Hokkaido and New England landscapes while celebrating Clark's career. Todd A. Richardson's (MLA, Class of 1987) proposal was selected for construction and the memorial dedicated in October 1991.

The artwork creates two outdoor rooms. A sculpted earthen berm, once the base of a reservoir constructed after the Clark house (which once stood on this site) burned down in 1890, marks off a small lawn. Among the trees at the site stands a large katsura believed to descend from a tree Clark brought from Hokkaido. Paired stones create a gateway to a second circular room enclosed with walls of painted rolled steel. The eastern curve depicts the Clark home, while its western counterpart features a silhouette of the Sapporo Clock Tower with the outlines visible from downtown Sapporo beyond. Visitors within this circle are intended to view these Hokkaido images against the backdrop of the UMass campus and our own hills beyond, a design that nods to the Japanese landscape and garden principle of "borrowed landscape." The large granite boulder within a pool of white pebbles at the memorial's center symbolizes Clark, the stone's height and angle suggesting "movement and energy out of the confines of the space, and into the future." [10] Narrow paths leading beyond the circle to sculptural wall fragments and more granite boulders create a sense of dynamism, stability, and conherence, while brass plaques commemorate highlights in Clark's career.

Richardson chose to work in stone because it "speaks without a language barrier" and because stones seem like "the bones of the earth. They're symbolic of a real connection to the land [and] Clark was about the land." The Memorial was recognized with a Merit Award from the American Society of Landscape Architects in 1992.

On April 30, 2001, Yamamoto Tadamichi, Consul General of Japan for New England, in a gesture commemorating the 125th anniversary of Clark's arrival in Japan, gave three cherry trees to the University. These were planted on the north side of the Clark Memorial and symbolize presidents William Wheeler and William Penn Brooks, as well as Professor David I. Penhallow, who accompanied Clark to Japan.

The Apiary in 1918

44. Apiary
1911

One of the last remnants of the lush market gardens, orchards, and vineyards that once filled this hillside, the Apiary sits quietly on the side of Clark Hill Road. It was, however, an essential part of those older landscapes, as the agricultural endeavors of the campus were dependent on pollination by bees. Furthermore, it is considered one of the first buildings in the country built exclusively for teaching about beekeeping. It is worth squinting and imagining a steep hillside of lawns, dotted with beehives.

Beekeeping had been a part of the curriculum of the MAC from early on in the college's history. But with the growth in sophistication of the field, College and Commonwealth officials thought it required a freestanding facility. In 1911 Burton N. Gates was appointed the state's "apiary inspector" and lecturer in beekeeping. Originally, the building contained a lab, library on beekeeping, and honey and wax extraction rooms. It also housed a small apartment upstairs for student tenants. Built on the southern side of the hill, close to the residential areas beyond the college's boundaries, the Apiary, like other laboratories at the MAC (such as East and West experiment stations) met a residential need even as it housed the latest scientific equipment and research.

Gates focused his research mainly on honey production, diseases, and issues related to pollination in the cucumber and cranberry industries so important to the region and state. After the 1969 retirement of the last professor of beekeeping, Frank R. Shaw, the beekeeping program declined in importance. But it never vanished completely. Today, the Apiary Laboratory is part of the Department of Plant, Soil, and Insect Sciences facilities and the building is currently used for research on medical entomology, including studies of pesticide effects on bees.

45. Fernald Hall
C. P. Hoyt, 1910

Among the most pressing topics in agriculture at the time of the MAC's founding was the problem of pests, which routinely destroyed crops. Entomology was included in the curriculum as early as 1868. In the 1880s, Charles Henry Fernald joined the faculty. A professor of zoology, Fernald in his research at the Agricultural Experiment Station studied the gypsy moth, browntail moth, spruce budworm, and San Jose scale. In time, Charles Fernald's son Henry Torsey Fernald joined his father on the faculty. Henry also succeeded Charles as associate entomologist at the Hatch Agricultural Experiment Station, and as director of the Graduate School at Massachusetts Agricultural College.

Fernald Hall

In time, MAC became one of the leading entomology programs in the region. As the department flourished a new home was needed. Fernald Hall was one of a number of research and teaching buildings planned and built under the leadership of Massachusetts Agricultural College President Goodell, who sought to improve the College's facilities.

Designed to house offices, laboratories and classrooms, museum space, and an auditorium for the Departments of Entomology and Zoology, Fernald Hall was dedicated on November 11, 1910. Built under the guidance of the younger Fernald, the building is a relatively conventional, symmetrical Georgian Revival style. Constructed of brick with stone trimmings, with heavily overhanging bracketed eaves and vertical strips of brick at the corners and windows, the building housed geological and mineralogical labs; zoology occupied the ground floor, and entomology above.

Fernald Hall originally held a zoological museum of 12,000 specimens, with space on the main floor for 16 cases; a geological museum with 6 cases; and an insect collection of over 100,000 specimens. It was a highlight of the campus, profiled, among other places, in the Works Progress Administration's 1937 guide to Massachusetts as one of the key reasons to visit Amherst, along with the homes of authors Emily Dickinson and Helen Hunt Jackson.

The entomology department's early twentieth-century interest in insect taxonomy was in time succeeded by other subjects, including insect behavior, physiology, and pest management. At the turn of the twentieth century entomology at UMass, now part of the Department of Plant, Soil, and Insect Sciences, moved toward evolution and genetics, with emerging interests in medical entomology, urban entomology, the role of insects in wild lands ecology, and the management of invasive species.

46. French Hall
James H. Ritchie, 1909–1918

Built to house the commercial floriculture and market gardening programs, French Hall (named for Henry Flagg French, first president of the Massachusetts Agricultural College) rose about the same time as Ritchie's other buildings across campus, Flint Laboratory and Stockbridge Hall. The two-story Georgian Revival building shares several features Ritchie chose for companion buildings across campus, including a granite foundation and bands running the length of the front elevation, a projecting central section, and a slate hip roof. The overall effect is elegant but reserved, which is altogether appropriate for this corner of campus where the eighteenth, nineteenth, and twentieth centuries come together.

47. Franklin Dining Hall / Permaculture Garden
Hugh Stubbins and Associates, Inc., 1965

The rapid increase in the size of the student body in the early 1960s and the growth of the Orchard Hill dormitories created demand for a new dining commons; the "South Commons"—later the Franklin Dining Commons—rose in a location convenient to both the dormitories just east of the academic buildings below.

For the building's design the University turned to Hugh Stubbins, architect of the Southwest Complex and Orchard Hill dormitories. Affectionately known as "the Copper Kettle" for its distressed copper roof canopy, which neatly hides electrical and air conditional equipment, the Franklin Dining Commons was considered a model of efficiency and modern design. Ramps leading up to the second-floor dining area from the east and west entrances were hailed for their effortless traffic flow.

Franklin continues the campuswide dialogue between modernist materials and design and more traditional New England wood and brick. The pre-aged copper canopy is a dramatic statement, and yet it rests on dark cut brick that gestures to Clark, French, Franklin, and Louis Warren Ross's neo-Georgian hillside dorms. But Stubbins's

Franklin Dining Hall

Permaculture garden

most effective move was not in selecting materials for the exterior, but rather in his interior choices. By raising up the dining hall and calling for wide, unbroken walls of glass on the second story, he provided a dignified, light-filled dining room for the thousands of students who have meals here each day.

More recently, the lawn on the west side of the dining hall has been converted to a permaculture garden, one of the first at a public university in the nation. Though it may seem today like an emerging idea, the term *permaculture* dates to 1909, when the American agronomist Franklin Hiram King, concerned with the impact American farming techniques was having on soil quality, traveled to Asia to study farming practices there. His 1911 book *Farmers of Forty Centuries* introduced the term *permanent agriculture*, today shortened to permaculture. Now, a century later, King's ideas are embraced by a thriving community of organic farmers. In October and November 2010, students spread over 250,000 pounds of organic matter by hand across the quarter-acre plot. In time, the garden will provide over 1,000 pounds of vegetables, herbs, fruit, and berries to the school's dining commons each year. In 2012 UMass Amherst sustainability manager Ryan Harb (BA '08; MA '10) and his team of fourteen students were honored by President Barack Obama at the White House as one of five "Champions of Change" recognized for outstanding leadership on campus.

1 João Pedro Almeida, *The Frank A. Waugh Arboretum: Challenges and Opportunities on an Evolving Landscape* (Amherst: University of Massachusetts Amherst, 2005).

2 "Benefit Calendar Lets You See the Forest and the Trees," *Boston Globe*, December 13, 2001.

3 Timothy O'Brien, "You Can't Get There From Here Anymore: A Partial History of Stockbridge Road, Amherst, Massachusetts," typescript, 2010 (Paynter Collection).

4 Kenyon Butterfield, as quoted in Harold Whiting Cary, *The University of Massachusetts: A History of One Hundred Years* (Amherst: University of Massachusetts Press, 1962), 110.

5 Eudora Van Meter Conant interview, February 2, 1977, SCUA.

6 "Distinguished Architecture for a State University," *Architectural Record* (May 1966), 170.

7 John Stifler, "Reprogramming Butterfield," *UMass Magazine Online* (Fall 2001), http://umassmag.com/Fall_2001.

8 Ibid.

9 "Certificate Program in Native American Indian Studies," last modified November 17, 2010, http://www.umass.edu/nativestudies.

10 This discussion, and quotation below, relies heavily on *The William Smith Clark Memorial* brochure, 8, RG 34, Series 104/C4, Box 1 Folder "Segments of Campus," SCUA.

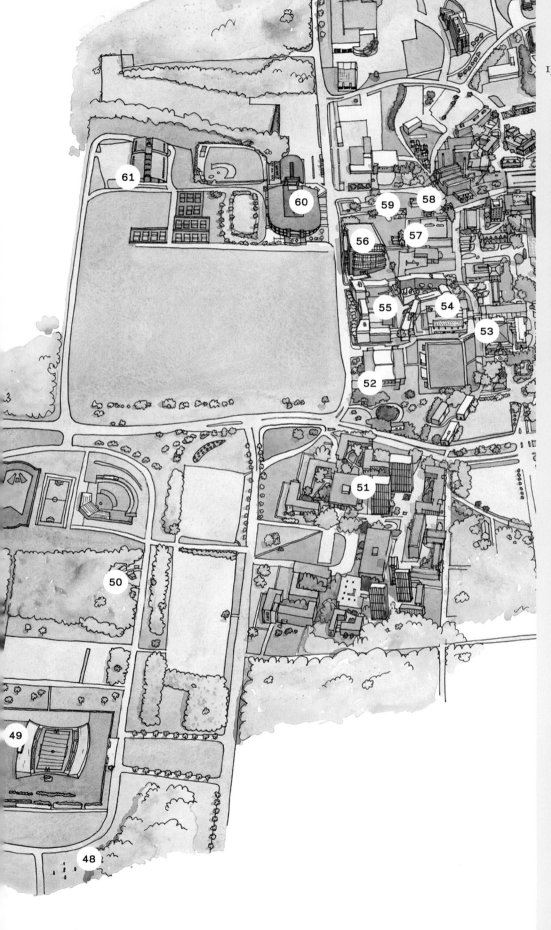

Walk Four: Southwest Campus & Commonwealth Avenue

This walk begins just off University Drive and proceeds north along Commonwealth Avenue through the Mill River floodplain; views to the west take in Hadley's Mount Warner, and the foothills of the Berkshires beyond. Once agricultural fields tilled by Hadley farmers, today the western edge of campus is home to facilities for most sports, including Warren McGuirk Alumni Stadium (football), Rudd Field (soccer), Lorden Field (baseball), the softball and track and field complexes, Garber Field (lacrosse), the Curry Hicks Cage, Boyden Gym, and the Mullins Center. The combination of the floodplain, perched water tables, wetlands, and silty substratum creates an area challenging for building development, but which has lent itself well to sports and recreational uses. The 1962 campus plan articulated this vision, largely realized today. The 2009 addition of the Recreation Center on the site of a large 1918 dairy barn made the transition from agriculture to athletics all but complete: the anticipated relocation of the 1894 Horse Barn from its site overlooking Commonwealth Avenue will further erase physical evidence of the University's origins.

The first athletic facility on the MAC campus was the Drill Hall, which began construction in 1882 on the current site of Bartlett Hall. The Drill Hall was initially built for military training, a mandatory element of the curriculum under the Morrill Land Grant Act of 1862. By the 1950s, physical education had become segregated by sex, with women sharing the increasingly fraying Drill Hall with the ROTC program, and men using the 1931 Curry Hicks Cage. A burgeoning campus population in the 1960s put increased strain on the athletic facilities, and the administration made plans for three projects, including a stadium and two other substantial athletic buildings. The Alumni Stadium, later renamed for longtime athletic director Warren McGuirk, Boyden Gym, and a basketball arena were the major projects planned.

The two newest athletic facilities feature heavily into the landscape of this part of campus now. The Mullins Center, which opened in 1993, is today host to the UMass basketball and hockey teams, and provides a venue for public ice skating as well as major music and theater productions. Across the street, the Recreation Center is home to the most up-to-date fitness equipment on campus. Its prominent placement along Commonwealth

Barn complexes like this one once defined the west edge of the campus. Today, only the Grinnell Arena (far right) survives on its original site; the horse barn just above is extant but will move to a new site to the northwest. The contemporary Commonwealth Avenue runs through the middle of the landscape shown here.

Avenue—once the site of MAC's night pastures—demonstrates the University's commitment to physical fitness among UMass students, faculty, and staff.

Commonwealth Avenue, which forms the main corridor along the west side of campus, was laid down as part of the 1961 master plan by Sasaki & Associates, one section of the ring road that moved the campus away from its agricultural roots into toward current urban design. If the era of the Sasaki plan was one that necessarily accommodated the nation's thriving car culture, more recent plans seek to advance alternatives. The Bikeway Connector, which enters campus at the South Gate near the Southwest Residential Area and runs along the length of University Drive, serves riders from the Norwottuck Rail Trail and Route 9, enabling many more employees, faculty members, and students to commute to campus on two wheels rather than four.

The Mullins Center

The Sunwheel

48. The Sunwheel

The University's answer to Stonehenge, the UMass Sunwheel is not in fact a replica of the ancient site on England's Salisbury Plain. Instead, this circular stone calendar, 130 feet in diameter, aims to educate both university students and the surrounding community about astronomy, in both past and present. Conceived by astronomy professor Judith S. Young, the installation is designed to provide an experiential basis for University students, schoolchildren, and the general public to learn about the movement of the sun.

First envisioned in 1992, construction of the Sunwheel began several years later when a dozen two-foot stones were placed at the site. A grant from the National Science Foundation as well as private donations over time funded the addition of fourteen 8-foot and 10-foot granite monoliths from the Chester Granite Co. in East Otis, Massachusetts, about 45 miles to the west in the Berkshires. Paired monoliths create the east and west portals, marking both the cardinal directions and the point of sunrise and sunset at the equinoxes, while a 10-foot high, 7,000-pound slab signals sunrise on the summer solstice. To keep the stones in place, 4-foot holes were lined with water-permeable fabric and filled with 51 tons of crushed stone; 2-foot stainless-steel pins and a coating of modern epoxy anchor each stone to its thick granite base.

The installation has drawn tens of thousands of visitors since 1999, as hundreds gather each year to attend seasonal sunrise and sunset gatherings, while area students and teachers visit the Sunwheel through the year to supplement school science curriculums.

Warren P. McGuirk Alumni Stadium

49. Warren P. McGuirk Alumni Stadium
Skidmore, Owings & Merrill, 1965[1]

Just north of the Sunwheel stands Warren P. McGuirk Alumni Stadium, a landmark of modernism on the UMass campus.

Athletics appeared at UMass almost as soon as the school was founded. The first class of some fifty Massachusetts Agricultural College students arrived in fall 1867, and the first sports team—baseball—formed the following year. Football arrived on the campus as early as 1878-79, when the "Aggies" in their inaugural game beat a team of Amherst College freshmen 4-0. By 1880 the campus had chosen its school colors, maroon and white. After the school was renamed the Massachusetts State College in 1931, the team was briefly called the Statesmen, but after the school officially became the University of Massachusetts in 1947, its sports teams were known as the Redmen, and the official mascot Chief Metawampe.

By 1960, the explosive growth of both the University and its football program generated support for the construction of a new sports facility. Land west of the central campus was purchased from Hadley dairy farmers James and Velma Kentfield, and planning began for a stadium. The siting of the new facility, at the edge of town and campus alike, aimed to mitigate the impact of crowds of students on the community.

The campus secured the firm Skidmore, Owings & Merrill to design the structure. Founded in Chicago in 1936 by Louis Skidmore and Nathaniel Owings (John Merrill joined in 1939), the firm would become instrumental in promoting the International Style "glass box" skyscraper; their work would include the Sears Tower (1973, the tallest in the world for over twenty years) and Burj Khalifa (2010, the world's tallest

Warren P. McGuirk Alumni Stadium, under construction

building as of this writing). David Childs of som is the architect of One World Trade Center at Ground Zero in New York City.

The architects conceived Alumni Stadium as a multipurpose facility that could be used for sports beyond football as well as the ceremonial occasions that punctuate university life. On August 27, 1964, the H. P. Madore Company of Southbridge, Massachusetts, began construction. The first major concrete stadium built in the Northeast since 1920, the venue boasted a capacity of 17,000. The stadium is one of the campus's midcentury gems, displaying the elegant simplicity of material and form that characterized the best works of the time. The stadium sits on a massive pad of concrete (necessary because of the soft soil of this lowland area) and appears at first to be square. But in fact, the two sides of seats are composed of two concave curves; the end zones are very slightly convex curves. And from the south and north, one sees a third curve, from the stop of one section of stands down to the field and back up to the other section.

The only element interrupting the sweep of the thick concrete walls on all sides is the almost free-floating rectangular press box on the west side. From a distance and from the air, the whole ensemble looks something like a Noguchi sculpture (perhaps not surprisingly, som's Gordon Bunshaft included a Noguchi sculpture in his design of Yale's Beinecke Library, completed in 1963, just a year before construction of McGuirk began).

As is true of other modernist building on campus, no effort is made to conceal the building's structural elements behind any cladding or veneer. An unusual feature is its raised design: the lowest seats in the stands are more than twelve feet off the ground. Indeed, the building is pure structure: seats are built into the concrete stands, and the rise of the stands makes way for the entrance ways into the stadium. There were neither doors nor any gates as part of the original design. The tall piers holding up the stands are surprisingly thin. As heavy as concrete is in the popular imagination, this building appears light and flexible. The concrete structure's bold curves and open spaces are the best expressions on the campus of this new material's possibilities.

The playing field itself was a notable feature at the time the stadium opened. Grass in the existing playing fields had been Rhode Island Bent, a variety with shallow roots that was easily ruined by cleats. When it opened in 1965, the new UMass field was blanketed with a pure Merion bluegrass that had been planted by the University's agronomy department four years earlier at their research facility in nearby South Deerfield, along the Connecticut River. A strain of seed valued for its close, springy quality as well as roots both deep and dense, Merion bluegrass was developed in the 1950s and had become a popular choice for sports stadiums.

Alumni Stadium hosted its first game on September 25, 1965, with the Redmen beating American International College, 41-0. The stadium was officially dedicated on October 16, 1965, when UMass defeated Rhode Island 30-7 during Homecoming. Graduation was held there for the first time in 1966.

By the mid-1970s, university administrators had begun to wish that the campus had an enclosed field for football as well as a facility for indoor soccer and indoor lacrosse. Talk turned to expanding the facility's usefulness by putting a dome over it. This Minute Dome (contemplated with the help of a feasibility study by Geiger Berger Associates, the firm that built, among other things, Detroit's Silver Dome) would involve a Teflon-treated covering pulled over a framework that consisted of a huge arch at the fifty-yard line and a series of interior steel cables, with steel support beams installed outside the field to hold the roof in place. Early plans also included solar panels, in hopes that federal funds for solar energy experimentation could be acquired. But the project was never realized, and alumni stadium remains an outdoor facility.

Although structurally the stadium has not changed, it is no longer the home of the Redmen. By the 1970s, increasing sensitivity to indigenous nations made the use of Native American–themed mascots controversial across the country. UMass proved no exception. In 1972, students were asked to choose a new mascot: their options were the Statesmen, the Artichokes, and the eventual winner, the Minuteman. The latter has not been without its own controversy, as members of the university community have suggested that the mascot, rifle in hand, promotes sexism, racism, and violence. In 2003, officials floated the notion of replacing the Minuteman with the gray wolf, but supporters of the Minuteman rallied and the proposal was abandoned.

In 1984, the stadium was renamed for Warren P. McGuirk, a longtime University athletic director who had played a major role in the stadium's design and construction. Another memorial gesture on this landscape is the Dallas Memorial Mall, across from the Stadium's east side, which honors Bernie Dallas (Class of 1966), a star athlete (and later member of the Philadelphia Bulldogs) killed in an automobile accident just two years after his graduation.

The question of how much the University would invest in its football program has bedeviled generations of leaders. Some, such as President J. Paul Mather (1953–60), saw the promotion of athletics as central to the expansion of the University. Others, such as Chancellor John V. Lombardi (2002–7), preached caution, noting football budgets' tendency to balloon, cutting into the core teaching and research functions of a university. In 2011, the campus administration of Chancellor Robert Holub (2008–12) chose to move UMass football into the Football Bowl Subdivision, the top division of the NCAA football leagues. A $54 million dollar stadium addition and renovation was launched as part of the requirements for moving into the new league.

50. Farley and Bowditch Lodges
Bernhard Dirks, 1933 and 1937

Originally located where Thompson Hall (1967) now stands, Bowditch Lodge (1937) was relocated to its current site in 1967, while Farley Lodge (1933) is believed to have been moved in about 1962. Documents of the University's thriving extension program, both single-story ranch-style cottages were constructed to house the Massachusetts State College's active 4-H Club community.

The construction of two 4-H lodges on the campus within just four years (1933–37), during the height of the Great Depression, reflects the Commonwealth's strong commitment to 4-H during the 1930s. The 4-H Movement is historically associated with the Extension Service of the U.S. Department of Agriculture and land-grant colleges and universities. While the mission of land-grant institutions such as UMass emphasized the development and dissemination of new agricultural knowledge, the adult audience for these innovations was not always receptive. Youth, though, proved more so, and could transmit their experiences to adults they knew. Launched in Ohio in 1902, the advent of 4-H in western Massachusetts can be traced to 1908, when some 500 Hampshire County schoolchildren were invited to join a "potato club" in which they learned about potato cultivation, tracked yields, and displayed successes.[2]

Both Bowditch and Farley lodges (the latter named for the father of 4-H in Massachusetts, George L. Farley) were designed and built by local volunteers from the 4-H community, who contributed some of the materials as well. Bernhard Dirks, a Greenfield architect with four small children who he hoped would one day join a 4-H Club, volunteered his services. Dirks, who practiced from the 1870s to the 1940s, had designed, among other things, the Town Hall (1878) in Bernardston, Massachusetts. Each lodge was designed in the New England summer cottage tradition, with the interior wood framing intentionally left exposed. The Bowditch Lodge building has a projecting front gable ell and a deep covered porch on its main, southeast elevation, sheltering the main entry. A massive fieldstone exterior chimney marks the building's southwest end. Foundation stones for Farley Lodge were recycled from old stone

Farley and Bowditch lodges

walls on Pelham Hill; the fireplace was built from stones retrieved from the Henry Fitts farm in Shutesbury, the stones broken open to expose the brilliant coloring inside. Opposite the fireplace was a small stage. A sun porch looked south and west, and enjoyed from its original location beautiful views of the Holyoke Range and foothills of the Berkshires. In the center of the hearth sat a stone presented by Anna McQueston Johnson (for whom Johnson Hall would be named in 1960; McQueston was a member of the UMass Advisory Council for Women from 1921 to 1944), which had been taken from a walk in West Street in neighboring Hadley. The town of Hadley had been among the first to embrace 4-H Club work, and the Johnson family—interested as they were in the past, present and future of agriculture—founded the Hadley Farm Museum in 1931 after moving the barn that currently houses it from Hadley's Porter-Phelps-Huntington property (in those years evolving from a private family home to a historic house museum) to the town center.[3]

Bowditch and Farley lodges also played a role in the University's early involvement with the Peace Corps, as they were used in 1962 to house early recruits who joined up shortly after President John F. Kennedy created the organization.

In time, both buildings were relocated to make room for the construction of Thompson Hall, their new site at the edge of the woods selected by Sasaki, Walker & Associates. Now associated with the Center for Early Education and Care, they are much altered and in part obscured by a utilitarian structure built to house campus childcare in the late 1990s.

51. Southwest Residential Area
Hugh Stubbins and Associates, 1966

The Southwest Residential Area, the largest of the campus dormitory communities, is home to about half of the on-campus undergraduate population. Among the most iconic structures at UMass Amherst, its five 22-story towers rise above eleven low-rise residence halls and two dining commons, together serving some 5,400 students. More people live in the Southwest Residential Area than reside in the neighboring town of Hadley just to the west.

The Southwest Residential Area reflects the massive growth UMass witnessed in the years following World War II. In 1964, the University acquired the land on which this dorm complex stands; fourteen families were displaced to make room for the massive new complex.

In selecting Hugh Stubbins, the University committed to the 52-year-old protégé of Walter Gropius, Marcel Breuer, and Alvar Aalto. Although schooled at the Graduate School of Design in the 1930s, when Walter Gropius, founder of the Bauhaus, was in charge, Stubbins soon pushed in new directions. Like other architects who came of age after World War II, Stubbins pursued a range of styles, and expanded the vocabulary of modernism. The onetime chair of the Department of Architecture at Harvard's Graduate School of Design, Stubbins had left teaching when his firm, founded in 1949, began to flourish. Over his career (he died in 2006), Stubbins designed over 800 buildings, in widely diverging styles. Before this UMass commission, Stubbins had made a name for himself first with his bold curving form for the Kongresshalle (1957) in West Berlin. He would go on to design, among other buildings, Veterans Stadium (1971) in Philadelphia, the Citigroup Center (1977) in New York, and the Ronald Reagan Library in Simi Valley (1988).

Stubbins had an impact on UMass as well as the Five Colleges. Elsewhere on the UMass campus he designed the Orchard Hill dormitories and the so-called Copper Kettle (Franklin Dining Hall). Stubbins had an even greater influence at nearby Hampshire College where, between 1968 and 1971, as creator of the campus's original master plan, he designed the core buildings of that new, experimental college: the Johnson Library Center (a building which, as architectural historian Paul F. Norton has noted, is "stylistically affiliated" with the Southwest dormitories, as a "similar play takes place between masses of dark, small-scale brick and large areas of whitish cement"), the Dakin (1969) and Merr II House (1970) dormitories, Franklin Patterson Hall (1970), and the Cole Science Center (1991). He also designed some ten buildings for Mt. Holyoke College, including Ham Hall (1965), the Alice Withington Rooke Laboratory Theatre (1966), and the Willits-Hallowell Center (1975).[4]

At UMass, Southwest's remoteness from the rest of campus allowed Stubbins to experiment with modern forms without clashing with the Georgian buildings elsewhere, although he nonetheless chose to clad the facades in brick of red-brown hue. The wide elevations of the towers (all but one face north and south) are composed of horizontal planes of brick, themselves framed by massive vertical piers of concrete,

A Southwest tower, shortly after opening

The bold lines of a Southwest low-rise

which run on the narrow sides of the building from ground to roof. On the faces, these dark surfaces yield to recesses and concrete again to signal the location of the public floors contained within the building's three 7-story "houses." While many wondered—as they would later about the Du Bois Library—why a rural campus would want to build skyscrapers for dormitories, for Stubbins it was clear: to accommodate the burgeoning student body and ensure that the campus remained walkable, the University would need to expand vertically. But Stubbins's goal was to re-create something like the house system of the older dorms, where a few hundred students would come to know each other well in the sea of a much larger university. Stubbins also worked hard to soften the impact on the landscape; the high-rise towers cannot be seen from the center of Amherst and are only partly visible from the higher elevations of the campus core.

However, from a distance, they are a dramatic statement, an indication, as *Architectural Record* opined in 1966, that "the University of Massachusetts is getting some architecture and knows where to put it." The magazine, insisting that "good campus design cannot be considered a luxury," praised UMass for providing an example of "distinguished architecture for a state university." [5]

Upon completion of the complex, four of the towers were named for Massachusetts-born U.S. presidents: John Adams, John Quincy Adams, Calvin Coolidge, and John F. Kennedy. An exception was made for the fifth tower, named for George Washington. A sixth tower was initially planned but was abandoned when funding fell short; by then, too, a number of students expressed skepticism about "elevator commuting." Several of the low-rise structures were named from New England authors, including Henry David Thoreau, Herman Melville, and Ralph Waldo Emerson, while others honored for figures from the University's past, like agricultural economics professor Alexander E. Cance and insect morphologist Guy C. Crampton.

As was true with Alumni Stadium, the complex afforded other specialists on campus the chance to try out new ideas. The Southwest Residential Area embraced instant landscaping, a technique developed by university landscape architect Walter A. Lambert that harnessed heavy earth-moving tools to plant mature shade trees. Mature sycamores were installed to line the pedestrian mall, while some forty-four pin oaks lining Fearing Street were planted in 1967 using this method, as were more than 170 red maples along University Drive.

Forty years later, an overhaul of the landscaping at Southwest, designed by Stephen Stimson Associates and implemented by Nauset Construction, was completed in 2011. The concourse reconstruction is a complete redesign of the pedestrian spaces of Southwest Residential Area and substantially increases the amount of green space there. In an effort to reflect the ecology of the Holyoke Range and the Pioneer Valley, only native plants and grasses were used. This project is one of the most sustainable that UMass has undertaken—when possible, materials from the old landscape were repurposed, including Pelham granite blocks salvaged from demolished MAC barns. Plantings were selected for drought tolerance, and much of the water used for irrigation will be recycled stormwater. The large benches stationed throughout the landscape are made from Ipê, a sustainably harvested hardwood.

The three largest spaces in the plan—the Washington, Hampden, and Berkshire decks—all employ the same materials but are configured to create a number of different atmospheres. The redesigned landscapes also seek to create intimate spaces, an effort to combat the crowds that often formed in the former open spaces at Southwest, contributing to the public safety issues that have plagued the complex.

The Southwest Residential Area is also home several of the campus's cultural centers, including the Latin American Cultural Center, the Malcolm X Cultural Center, and the Stonewall Center, an important resource for the local LGBTQ community and a leader in the development of campus resources for sexual minorities. At the time of its creation it was only the third center of its kind on an American college campus. A series of homophobic incidents in 1984 followed by protests led to the development of a report on the campus climate for lesbian, gay, and bisexual students that recommended, among other things, the creation of the Program for Gay, Lesbian, and Bisexual Concerns. The program, established in 1985, later was renamed The Stonewall Center: A Lesbian, Bisexual, Gay, and Transgender Educational Resource Center (a reference to the Greenwich Village bar and the violence that ensued there after a 1969 police raid). Today, the Center's programs provide support and advocacy for LGBTQ and allied students, staff, and faculty at UMass Amherst and for the greater Pioneer Valley.

Hampden Dining Hall and the tower of Southwest

Boyden Gym

52. Boyden Gym
Morris W. Maloney, 1963

By the mid-twentieth century, campus athletic facilities, designed to support a male enrollment of about 500, were serving some 1,500 students. At the time of its construction, Boyden Gym, built to house men's physical education programs, promised to be one of the finest facilities of its kind in the country. Maloney's Totman Gym for women had already been completed, four years earlier. Boyden's basketball and squash courts, large gymnasium, labs for physiology and physiotherapy, six-lane swimming pool, weight room, and locker rooms—even eight fully equipped ten-pin bowling alleys—were planned to serve some 6,000 students.

Completed in February 1964, the exterior of the four-floor structure was constructed of brick, aluminum, and glass, chosen for their durability. The building was designed with the main stairwells located on the four outer corners of the building to divert foot traffic away from the building's core. A multicolored panel on the north elevation seems to glow when the building is internally illuminated at night, a delightful surprise in an otherwise restrained exterior. Architect Morris W. Maloney of Springfield, who had worked on (among other things) the East Longmeadow foundry of the New England Steel Casting Company and the St. Agnes School in Dalton, Massachusetts, had developed a focus on school design. In addition to the gym, Maloney also designed the 1953 Worcester Dining Commons and would soon contribute the 1966 addition to the Morrill Science Center, which straddles the east-west exterior passageway.

Named in honor of Frank L. Boyden, a renowned educator best known as the headmaster of nearby Deerfield Academy from 1902 to '68 (and the subject of John McPhee's book *The Headmaster*), the building honors this longtime UMass trustee and chair of the Board of Trustees through the 1960s. The pool in Boyden Gym is dedicated to beloved swimming coach Joseph Rogers, who taught Physical Education from 1930 until 1975. His involvement helped swimming become a varsity sport in 1935 and he retired with a 152–149 meet record. Rogers's background in engineering made him a sought-after consultant in pool design and construction. He helped plan numerous high school and college projects as well as the aquatic facilities at the United States Air Force Academy in Colorado Springs.

53. Curry Hicks

Clinton F. Goodwin of Morse and Dickinson Engineers, 1931; addition: Childs Bertman Tseckares & Casendino, 1984

Behind Boyden Gym, on the other side of Garber Field, stands Curry Hicks "Cage," among other things the longtime home of UMass basketball. Invented in 1891 by James. A. Naismith in Springfield, twenty-five miles to the south, basketball is today a hallmark of local culture; the hemispheric dome of the Naismith Memorial Basketball Hall of Fame (Gwathmey Siegel Associates Architects, 2002) welcomes thousands of visitors each year. So it is unsurprising that the campus has long nurtured an interest in the sport, though it got off to a surprisingly slow start. By 1899 Professor Richard Swann Lull had suggested the old Drill Hall be used as a gymnasium, and it was subsequently modified for use by the college's first basketball and indoor track teams. The Drill Hall stood on the site currently occupied by Bartlett Hall until its demolition in 1958.

The first varsity basketball team hit the court in 1902 and began their career with an 18–12 loss to Amherst College on January 18th, though they soon had success over Trinity College with a 16–14 win. The fledgling sport had difficulty gaining ground on campus, however, and when it still failed to attract an audience basketball was dropped as a varsity sport. Athletic director Curry Hicks, hired in 1911, took an interest in the game and reinstated it during the 1916–17 academic year. He hired alumnus Harold M. "Kid" Gore, Class of 1911, to coach the team. Gore stayed on as coach for eleven seasons, ending with a record of 85-53. The next coach, Fritz Ellert, guided the team through four seasons with a record of 38-19.

Interior, Curry Hicks "Cage"

By the late 1920s, Curry Hicks had set his sights on a new facility to house basketball and other athletics at UMass, and he worked tirelessly with the alumni to fund and build the original 1931 section of this recreation building. The architect, Clinton Goodwin, had been a member of MAC's Class of 1916 and was charged with creating a building that would house a complete indoor and outdoor program usable through the entire academic year.

Hicks and Goodwin worked out the plan for the building, including a glass roof with louvered vent panels and a "cage" that included a running track, pool, basketball floor, baseball infield, and 2,500 seats for spectators. The original dirt track has since been covered with gymnasium flooring. On the exterior, the original Classical Revival building has a mixture of Renaissance elements that include the arch and broken pediment in the center of the east facade. The postmodern 1984 addition by Childs, Bertman, Tseckares and Casendino to the south repeats the scheme of the pediment in a central glass skylight that extends downward to the entrance doors. The addition provided a public entrance to the cage and contains a ticket booth, locker rooms, and offices.

The building served its core purposes well. The 1961–62 team was the first to be invited to take part in the NCAA tournament, and by the 1960s and early 1970s, had attracted nationally ranked played such as Julius "Dr. J" Erving (who enrolled in 1968, majoring in personnel management, and lived in Southwest's Kennedy Tower). Erving's presence had a big impact on the popularity of the team and lines formed outside cramped Curry Hicks to see him play. Campus leadership credited a winning season and run-up to the NIT with cooling campus down after the Mills House takeover (see Walk Five).

Indeed, politics infused the athletic facility just as it had other places on campus. Spring 1970 was a dramatic semester for protests and resistance movements, including the February 18th occupation of Mills House. On Thursday, February 19th, black students took over buildings at Mount Holyoke College and Amherst College. Meanwhile, the Chicago Seven, accused of having incited riots at the 1968 Democratic Convention (where the party nominated Vice President Hubert Humphrey for president), were found guilty. Tensions were high when Humphrey arrived just days later to speak in the UMass Cage on foreign policy. Humphrey was drowned out when between 4,500 and 5,000 students, including 400 to 500 demonstrators, arrived and began to harangue him. Humphrey eventually abandoned his speech and left (he afterwards met with a delegation of students at his hotel, and talked with them late into the night). The then chancellor Oswald Tippo was mortified, but Humphrey, having experienced this before and perhaps familiar with the strong passion for political activism among the student population, was unfazed: "Don't give it another thought," he said. "I have been through this a hundred times." [6]

As the largest gathering space until the construction of the Mullins Center, the Cage also sheltered important events on campus. One of the most popular was the Annual Horticultural Show, which converted the entire floor building into a sea of mature tree, shrub, and grass landscapes; miniature gardens; and educational booths, all erected and staffed by students, faculty, and staff. The show was a major attraction in the region and was still held in the late 1950s. The Cage also hosted many musical headliners before the Mullins Center opened, including Joan Baez and Johnny Carson.

Of course, basketball was its primary purpose. Jack Leaman proved the program's winningest coach, with 217 victories. Following several down seasons after Leaman's 1978 retirement, the Minutemen rebounded under new coach John Calipari, who arrived in 1988. Under Calipari, the team became A-10 Tournament champions five consecutive years (1991–96) and played in the NCAA Tournament seven times, appearing twice in the Elite Eight (1995, 1996) and once in the Final Four (1996). The Cage remained the home of men's basketball from its opening until 1993, when the team moved to the Mullins Center.

54. Tobin Hall
Coletti Brothers, 1972

This seven-story concrete building opened in fall 1972, during a season of major construction. That year, the UMass *Index* noted that the "The Shortest Distance Between Two Points...Is Undoubtedly Under CONSTRUCTION." During the 1971–72 academic year, several projects were in various stages of completion, including the new twenty-eight-story library and the Fine Arts Center. Lederle Graduate Research Center had also been recently completed.

Tobin Hall, planned to house the study of psychology and considered the "second addition to Bartlett," was conceived by Coletti Brothers, who had recently contributed the design for Herter Hall. The building's placement can cause it to be easily overlooked today, but it was a strong addition to the modernist landscape emerging in

Tobin Hall

the early 1970s, when its stylistic relationship to nearby Herter Hall and the Whitmore Administration Building was readily apparent (and still visible today from Massachusetts Avenue). The firm's design echoed choices made in their earlier contribution to the campus. Long appreciative of the sculptural possibilities of concrete, the firm again embraced the geometric power of deep concrete coffers. The heavy mass of the office and classroom spaces rests on 26 huge octagonal columns, making lighter what otherwise would be a pure block of concrete. The effect was enhanced by placing vertical spans of windows where sharp corners would otherwise be, and by projecting three-stories of the office slab out to the most visible, west side. Indeed, from Commonwealth Avenue to the west, the building appeared almost delicate, like it was lightly balanced on a narrow hilltop. At the same time, a series of terraced garden spaces built into the slope beneath the east elevation integrated the building into the landscape. Tobin Hall is now largely hidden by the massive new Commonwealth Honors College complex.

55. Commonwealth Honors College Residential Complex
William Rawn Associates, 2013

As early as the 1890s, students embraced the opportunity to work toward "honors" in their studies: in 1894, 23 undergraduate honors theses were archived in the library. Some of the first works included "English Agriculturists: A Study in Sociology," by Robert F. Pomeroy, "The Dehorning of Cattle," by H. D. Hemenway, and "The Development of Rapid Fire Guns and their Role in Modern Warfare," by Henry J. Fowler. As the Massachusetts Agricultural College grew into the Massachusetts State College and then the University of Massachusetts, more departments offered honors opportunities for their students. The first campuswide Honors Program was created in 1960, with honors courses available not only in the arts and sciences, but also in the professional schools. By the late 1970s, some 400 students were enrolled in the Honors Program; over the following decade that number grew to 600. In the mid-1990s, the Massachusetts Board of Higher Education proposed an honors college for the Commonwealth of Massachusetts, and Commonwealth College welcomed its first official class in the fall of 1999. Today, Commonwealth Honors College serves about 3,000 students in 88 majors.

In response to that growth, campus leaders decided to create a cluster of buildings dedicated to Honors programs. Plans for a new living/learning facility sited on the east side of Commonwealth Avenue between the Recreation Center and the Boyden Gymnasium call for buildings ranging from four to six stories arranged around a series of courtyards. The complex will house 1,500 students, and contain nine classrooms, a cafe, laundry facilities, and administrative offices of the Honors College. It will also contain faculty and staff apartments, an arrangement that had been prevalent in dormitories in the past, but had slowly dwindled as fewer professors maintained an interest in living on campus. It is one of the largest projects at the University in decades, totaling about a half-million square feet. Following through on the campus sustainability initiative, the project will seek certification at the LEED Silver level or better.

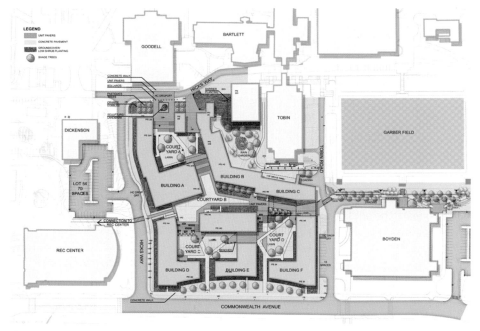

Commonwealth Honors College

To tackle this landmark landscape-within-a-landscape, the campus turned to William Rawn, the architect perhaps best known as the designer of the South Amherst dwelling portrayed in Tracy Kidder's 1985 nonfiction account of its construction, *House*. Rawn's firm has built widely praised public buildings as well, such as Seiji Ozawa Hall at Tanglewood (1994, the summer home to the Boston Symphony Orchestra) in Lenox, Massachusetts, the '62 Center for Theatre and Dance (2005) in Williamstown, Massachusetts, and the Cambridge Public Library (2010).

Rawn and his team of architects have had a number of goals in this large and challenging site. In keeping with the long history here of respecting and engaging the power of the land itself, they have tried to take advantage of a steep, thirty-five-foot grade change from the top (behind Bartlett) to the bottom of the site (adjacent to Boyden Gym and Commonwealth Avenue) to preserve views westward toward Mount Warner and the surrounding hills while creating outdoor spaces that are essential to building a sense of community. Toward that end, the tallest buildings are at the top of the site, and the shortest at the bottom.

The design strengthens the urban feel of the campus by reinforcing the line of Commonwealth Avenue on the west side of the site and Hicks Way on the north. But this is not a fully enclosed college like those found at Harvard and Yale. The architects have emphasized the natural pathways of the campus, encouraging students to pass through the complex and its green spaces on their way to the Recreation Center or to the library and the main classroom buildings from Southwest and the athletic fields. The buildings have a strong formal similarity to the Wieland and King residence halls (2004) that the firm contributed to nearby Amherst College (including the gentle curve of the buildings along Commonwealth Avenue and Hicks Way), even though red brick was chosen for the Commonwealth College in place of the granite at Amherst College. The curve of this building is echoed in other projects across campus, such as the new Laboratory Science Building just east of North Pleasant Street. The return to the use of brick as the mainstay material here and elsewhere across campus in recent years in this design has been joined with a break from rigidly orthogonal buildings.

56. Recreation Center
Sasaki Associates, 2009

The Recreation Center stands on land that was once home to one of the campus's several farm complexes, remnants of the agricultural college days. A similarly state-of-the-art facility once stood on this site—a 1918 stucco cow barn, its soaring interior enclosed with thick fire walls—that also reflected the college's earlier commitments to cutting-edge technologies, in this case features like automatic feeders and other assets to modern dairy production. Controversy over whether the administration gave proper notice concerning the demolition of the barn energized a group of current and retired staff and faculty to bring attention to historic preservation issues on campus. Out of

Dairy barns on the site of the Recreation Center

The state-of-the-art rec center claimed the site of a turn-of-the-century agricultural facility; its demolition sparked the launch of Preserve UMass.

Recreation Center Atrium

that came Preserve UMass (PUMA), an organization dedicated to promoting a serious debate about how to balance past, present, and future. After some delays, the project continued as planned with the removal of the stucco dairy barn. But the campus administration was pressured to undertake a serious examination of its historic resources and give greater consideration to the historic buildings and landscapes on the campus.

Construction of the Recreation Center, designed by Sasaki Associates, began in 2007. The red brick exterior aims to cue associations not only with the Mullins Center across the street but also the nineteenth-century buildings at the heart of the campus center. The brick surface is broken by deep reveals at openings, emphasizing solidity, in contrast to lighter and cleaner surfaces of bright aluminum and glass. The natural light-filled atrium opens into a concourse that stretches through the building, offering communal spaces, including informal seating and an amphitheater.

57. Grinnell Arena
1911

George N. Parks Minuteman Marching Band Building
Kuhn Riddle Architects, 2011

Grinnell Arena was built in 1911 as an animal husbandry building and livestock judging arena. In 1929, the Abattoir Slaughter House rose on the west side. Together, these two buildings—both part of the Brooks Farm Complex, a series of buildings that were intended to serve as the center of livestock husbandry for the College—represented a continuation of the trustees' commitment to upgrade the College's physical plant with modern agricultural and teaching facilities. The Arena was once home to two significant animal attractions in the region—the Bay State Dairy Classic and the Little International Livestock Show. Other buildings in this group include the extant 1894 Horse Barn and Blaisdell House, as well as a number of barns and ancillary structures, including a farmhands' dormitory/milkers' bungalow, a dairy complex, and a silage storage building. The Brooks Farm Complex continued to function as a center of livestock husbandry for the University into the 1960s when many agricultural operations were relocated to new facilities in East Deerfield, Massachusetts.

Today the buildings are associated with another UMass institution: the UMass Minutemen Marching Band. Though the history of band music here finds its origins in the Morris Drum Corps, a fife and drum band formed in the late nineteenth century, the marching band dates to 1935, when it was organized under the direction of Charles Farnum. Under the memorable direction of George N. Parks, who came in UMass in 1977, the band became known as "The Power and Class of New England."

Beginning in the 1950s, the band used the Old Chapel as their rehearsal venue, but in time, the Chapel was allowed to deteriorate, and the band relocated to the Grinnell Arena. Fifteen years later the band gained approval for its own building, designed by Kuhn Riddle Architects, a local firm that has given many UMass architecture students their first internships and jobs (Kuhn Riddle also guided the redesign and reconstruction of the plaza of the Fine Arts Center, and designed the New Student Center addition to Marcus Hall, one of the principal buildings of the Engineering Quadrangle). The 2-story 15,000-square-foot brick-clad facility building the architects designed is connected to Grinnell Arena and contains a 5,500-square-foot rehearsal hall that accommodates the full marching band of some 400 students as well as the necessary staff offices, practice rooms and support spaces.

George Parks died suddenly in September 2010 as the band was en route to Ann Arbor for a weekend performance. The building was to be named for Parks even before his tragic death, in honor of his tremendous leadership, but the building now serves as a memorial to this important campus figure. In his 30-plus-year career at UMass, Parks was awarded the Distinguished Teaching Award, the Chancellor's Medal for service to the campus, and an Award for Outstanding Accomplishments in Scholarly and Creative Activity. Under Park's guidance, in 1998 the band received the Louis C. Sudler Trophy from the John Philip Sousa Foundation, the nation's top marching band honor.

Grinnell Arena and the George N. Parks Minuteman Marching Band Building

58. Blaisdell House
1869

Blaisdell House

One of a handful of residences on campus, this two-and-a-half-story wood-frame Greek Revival house, with its side gable roof rear ell, and familiar front porch embellished with an octagonal pavilion at its southeast corner, is a rare survivor from the earliest days of the campus. In fact, Blaisdell House is now considered the oldest extant University building on the campus (though it is not on its original site), a rare artifact of those years before the graduation of the "Pioneer Class of 1871."

Originally located on Lincoln Avenue, and occupied in the 1870s by farm superintendent John C. Dillon and a number of students, the house was moved to its current site in 1893. Later it became home to Grace and Fred Cooley, the latter having to come to UMass from Bozeman, Montana, where he directed the state college experiment station there. Cooley would be responsible, among other things, for the dam that created the Campus Pond.

In April 1946, Matthew Blaisdell (MAC Class of 1929), assistant professor of animal husbandry and farm superintendent, brought his family (his wife Ida and sons John and Raymond) to live on the campus. The Blaisdells were there for some twenty-eight years, until 1974. Today the house, no longer surrounded by the farm complex it once looked out over, shelters university offices.

59. Horse Barn
F. F. Gilman, 1894

During the 1890s and into the early twentieth century, Massachusetts State College started restructuring its facilities and the layout of campus to better suit the needs of a growing student body and their demands for expanded academic and agricultural facilities.

Built as a "model barn" (with funds provided to the Massachusetts Agricultural College by the General Court) this picturesque, one-and-half-story horse barn, with its hip roof, large off-center open passageway, roof dormers in its east and west elevations, and double-leaf barn doors, offers an appealing example of Queen Anne architecture on the campus. Contrasting surface treatments (including clapboards, vertical trim boards, shingled gable peaks, and curved siding in the gable returns alongside decorative woodwork and windows stacked above the south elevation's barn doors) provide this long barn facade with a visual feast of elements that break up the surfaces and enliven the building's appearance. Curved wooden scrolls flanking the vertical board panels "direct the eye inward and upward from the outer edges of the broad barn

The 1894 horse barn

doors to the narrower board panels over-head, then up through the fixed windows over the board panels, and then finally through three freestanding vertical boards that stick out above the window, into a visual endpoint at the roofline of the gable peak."[7]

The barn originally housed the College's Percheron workhorses, which had provided the power needed to clear some four hundred acres to make forage space for the farm's 450 head of cattle. In the 1940s, after the federal government disbanded the U.S. Cavalry, the barn became the stable for Morgan horses (the Percherons having been sold in the 1950s to finance expansion of the academic program, signaling the University's shifting priorities); the barn is considered to have been the home of the original Bay State Morgan bloodline, a distinguished breeding line in the equestrian world.

The Horse Barn remained in full use until 1991, when the Morgan horses were relocated to the University's farm in Hadley. Threatened for the past two decades with demolition, the University, with support from the Massachusetts Farm Bureau Federation, now plans to move the barn together with Blaisdell House just north of the campus and turn both into an Agricultural Learning Center.

60. Mullins Center
Robert Galloway, Cambridge Seven Associates, 1993

By the mid-1980s, the student population at the University of Massachusetts had grown to 24,000 students. Men's sports were still being played in the Curry Hicks Cage, which sat only 4,200 and hockey had been discontinued for lack of an appropriate venue. At this point, State Representative and sports enthusiast William D. Mullins began a campaign to gain support for a new sports arena.

The legislative bill that funded the facility named it as the "Mullins Convocation Center," so that like the Fine Arts Center, it would not be seen by the public as a threat to the Springfield Civic Center. Unlike in the Roche building, Cambridge Seven was able to incorporate the necessary support spaces and rigging for large concerts and productions, including a sally port that can hold two tractor trailers, numerous dressing rooms, and a green room, as well as home and visiting team locker rooms for basketball, football, and hockey and team support spaces. The Mullins Center has been the venue for music concerts from Metallica to Bob Dylan and shows from the Ice Capades and *Jesus Christ Superstar* to Cirque du Soleil.

A complex of livestock barns, including the Sheep Barn, was razed in September 1990 to make way for the new arena. Awarded the 1994 Merit Award by AIA New England, the Center is the home of UMass basketball and hockey, and it serves as a public skating rink, a concert hall, and a center for other ceremonial occasions, not

The south elevation of Mullins Center

only for the University but for the whole Pioneer Valley. This brick building is sensitively designed to avoid a bulky appearance, in part by deploying a low-slung metallic roof.

The public skating rink is a separate, yet integrated, structure. Distinctive red and white light standards anchor the north and south facades of the main structure, and even such mundane features as downspouts are well incorporated into the overall design. Hockey has also had a long history at UMass, beginning with a December 1908 victory over Springfield Tech. The distinguished 1921 hockey team boasted of two silver medalists at the 1924 Chamonix Olympics in the French Alps: Jerry McCarthy and John Lions (7 of 10 from Massachusetts). The Campus Pond provided the team's only facilities until 1939, where the hockey team played off and on until it resumed as a regular sport in 1954 and the team played at Amherst College's Orr Rink. The teams found it too hard to share space, though, and hockey was put on pause for more than two decades after 1979. Campus officials had been thinking about building a rink since the late 1940s, but the idea did not succeed until this plan for an integrated complex for multiple sports gained traction.

The third floor of the Mullins Center houses the University's Athletic Hall of Fame, founded in 1969 to celebrate the accomplishments of university athletes. A scarcity of funding led to a lull in additions since 1982, but a donation from former star basketball player George "Trigger" Burke has funded the hall since 1996.

The Central Heating Plant

61. Central Heating
R. G. Vanderweil Engineers with Cambridge Seven Associates, 2008

From its early days of Massachusetts Agricultural College, some buildings were heated with their own steam boilers and lit with gas lights. The first building to be electrified was the 1894 Brooks Barn. This first "dynamo" in the basement of the dairy barn was far from safe and efficient—its short chimney did not provide adequate ventilation and resulted in an interior covered in soot. Also in the 1890s, electricity (provided by the Town of Amherst Gas and Electric Company) was added to the Chapel and North and South colleges.

In the 1940s, a coal-fired steam plant was installed in the ravine west of the campus center, its three towering stacks becoming a visual landmark on campus. West Virginia coal burning at some 2,400 degrees Farenheit heated rooms across campus. Then, late in 1973, in order to comply with stricter air pollution regulations, a three-story oil-powered heating plant was opened off Tillson Farm Road to replace the original coal-powered plant. There were severe problems with the joints in the pipes, however, and they proved unable to contain the high pressure steam from the plant. The plant was in operation for several months in the winter of 1976 until the problems were discovered and the University was forced to return to using the old steam plant. Because the plant never worked properly, the University did not accept it from the State Division of Capital Planning Operation (DCPO), and though alternative uses for the space, such as offices and classrooms were investigated, it remains vacant. Perhaps its greatest legacy is the urban legend the incident launched, another among the campus classics: many people (erroneously) believe that university planners failed to account for the plant's siting, overlooking the inability of steam to travel downhill.

After a hundred years of use, campus planners decided that the power plant had become too inefficient and costly to maintain, and could not be expanded to meet the needs of the projected building boom of the first two decades of 2000. Planning was begun for a new, more sustainable power plant. The new plant was designed by Cambridge Seven Associates in collaboration with R. G. Vanderweil Engineers of Boston, BSC Group, McNamara/Savlia, Haley and Aldrich of Boston, and Earth Tech of Concord. The facility, which bears almost no resemblance to coal power plants of the past, is a dramatic addition to the campus and serves as the symbol of the University's nationally recognized commitment to a more energy-efficient campus. UMass has garnered numerous awards for its growing list of sustainable practices, including a dedication to meeting LEED standards for new buildings, subsidizing the free bus system, and emphasizing local food production and recycling. The Central Heating Plant is a 45,000-square-foot building with a 95,000-square-foot curved roof that elegantly covers the facility and a variety of storage tanks. It is inspired by athletic field houses and plays off the curved roof line of the Mullins Center just to the east. It is the cleanest power plant of its size in New England and has had a remarkable 80 percent efficiency in its first years of operation. Because of this efficiency—achieved by turning steam heat created by the initial production process into more energy—the plan has helped reduce the campus greenhouse gas emissions by approximately 75 percent. A prominent chimney spews not toxic pollution but rather a pure white smoke that is only nitric oxide and water vapor.

In 2012, the old coal-fired steam plant was demolished; plans are in place to create on its site an intermodal transit center that will emphasize the use of buses and bicycles.

1 The University has long identified the stadium as having been designed by Gordon Bunshaft of SOM. Early accounts of the building note that he was a consulting designer, however McGuirk was not claimed by him as one of his designs, nor is it included in surveys of his work.

2 Franklin M. Reck, "The 4-H story: A History of 4-H club work," (Ames, Iowa: Iowa State College Press, 1951).

3 The Hadley Farm Museum, just east of the intersection of routes 9 and 47 in Hadley, is still open to the public today. Likewise, the Forter-Phelps-Huntington Museum at 130 River Drive in Hadley continues to interpret the history of the family and community. Anna McQueston Johnson's husband was the notable author and photographer Clifton Johnson; much of his work memorialized rural life in New England and elsewhere.

4 Paul F. Norton, Amherst: A Guide to Its Architecture (Amherst: Amherst Historical Society, 1975), 115.

5 "Distinguished Architecture for a State University," Architectural Record (May 1966), 168.

6 Irving Seidman, Oswald Tippo and The Early Promise of the University of Massachusetts: A Profile in His Own Words (Amherst: University of Massachusetts Amherst, 2002), 69–70.

7 W. Maros, C. Weed, and C. Beagan, Massachusetts Historical Commission, AMH.103, May 2009.

North Campus

Walk Five: North Campus

This Walk, which starts at Stockbridge Hall and travels through the north end of campus and concludes at the Gunness Engineering Student Center, takes in the growth of the sciences on the twentieth-century campus, beginning with the advent of agricultural engineering and ending with the modern engineering campus. Today this constellation of buildings houses the College of Engineering, the College of Natural Sciences, and the Stockbridge School of Agriculture—a thriving range of departments that all trace their origins to our history as an institution devoted to agricultural innovation.

Some of the oldest extant buildings associated with that story today stand just north of the Murray D. Lincoln Campus Center. Although oriented in an irregular pattern now, several of the structures encountered here—West Experiment Station, East Experiment Station, Draper Hall, Flint Laboratory, Stockbridge Hall, and Goessmann Laboratory—were constructed between 1885 and 1922 along the north side of what was once Olmsted Road (later Ellis Drive). A tree-lined road that curved around the west side of the pond, connecting to North Pleasant Street at both its northern and southern ends, Olmsted Road was removed between 1959 and 1973 as the campus embraced a more modern, urban aesthetic. The ground southeast of these buildings was historically an open lawn leading to the Campus Pond; as space was filled by the Student Union (1957) and Campus Center (1970), the visual connection between the Olmsted Road buildings and the Campus Pond vanished.

As early as the 1890s, the Trustees had determined that the continued growth of the Massachusetts Agricultural College as an institution demanded a substantial reorganization in terms of land use. The new dormitories and lecture halls that were so urgently needed would most obviously be sited within the core campus, where the College's agricultural facilities were already located. Meanwhile the existing layout was becoming inconvenient for farmers, not least because of the excessive time and expense involved in moving materials from fields to barns that had or would become scattered among non-farm campus buildings. In a series of decisions, the Trustees sought to create more purposeful and practical academic and agricultural landscapes.

The Trustees also saw the challenge of relocating the farms as an opportunity to create new, sanitary, model barns and veterinary laboratories where hard-to-eradicate problems (such as tuberculosis among livestock) might be addressed. The initial farm buildings that once stood where Herter Hall is today gave way to new complexes to the west. During the 1890s and into the twentieth century, new state-of-the-art agricultural facilities were built, including the Hatch Laboratory (1891), Horse Barn (1894), Munson Hall (1898, the first Paige Veterinary Laboratory), and the Munson Hall Annex.

At the same time, the growth of the engineering curriculum and faculty prompted other changes. Though engineering was present on campus from

North Campus, the heart of the science programs

MAC's beginning, after the 1914 construction of Stockbridge Hall, engineering and the physical sciences came to dominate the northern edge of the campus. In 1915 the school developed a Department of Rural Engineering, offering courses on farm structures and machinery; agricultural engineering received a dedicated home that same year, when the single-story building today at 250 Natural Resources Road was erected. Twenty years later, engineering activities on campus were combined into a single Department of General Engineering. But soon the department was divided again, into departments of Agricultural and Civil Engineering. With the influx of World War II veterans eager to take advantage of the G.I. Bill, pressure mounted for a full-scale school of engineering. In 1947, that school was established, with four departments: Agricultural, Civil, Electrical, and Mechanical Engineering. A department of Chemical Engineering was added in 1948.

The early twentieth century saw a watershed moment at UMass and on the north campus in 1918 when Walter W. Chenoweth, with help from Frank Waugh and Sears, founded the Department of Horticultural Manufacturing— that is, the nation's first food science department. Prompted by an acute interest in food production and preservation during World War I, this new endeavor was first housed in Flint Laboratory; in 1930 Chenoweth Laboratory rose on the slope west of Stockbridge Hall, providing the department a dedicated home.

The college's emphasis on science continued in the mid-twentieth century as facilities expanded to house other departments. The laboratory complex, including Gunness Laboratory (which rose in 1949, the first building dedicated specifically to engineering), Marston Hall (1950), Paige Laboratory (1950), the

Holdsworth Hall   *Agricultural Engineering Center*

Animal Isolation Laboratory (1953), and Thayer Animal Disease Laboratory (1957) emerged between 1949 and 1957 in the former agricultural fields to the north of Draper Hall. The 1963 construction of Holdsworth Hall—built to house Forestry and Wildlife Management (and today the home of the Department of Environmental Conservation)—the 1966 addition to Chenoweth Lab and the 1967 appearance of Agricultural Engineering Center further expanded capacity.

Other engineering programs grew and flourished. The industrial engineering program began in 1966, followed soon after by mechanical engineering and, in time, aerospace engineering. In 1972, electrical engineering expanded to include computer engineering. In 1961, the creation of the Polymer Research Institute was the first step toward the development of today's highly ranked Polymer Science and Engineering Department, engaging more than two hundred scientists and students.

With the building of Governor's Drive (which together with Commonwealth Avenue and Massachusetts Avenue encircle campus), the northern edge of the university gained definition. In recent years, the campus has also witnessed increased development between the core of the campus and the laboratory complex. New buildings include the Gunness Engineering Student Center (1985) and the Knowles Engineering Building (1991). Together with Marston Hall, these buildings defined a new quadrangle to the south of the laboratory complex.

Today, the College of Engineering at UMass Amherst is ranked the best public engineering school in New England, and the department of food science is the number-one doctoral program in that field. The College of Natural Sciences and the fifteen departments housed within it (as well as the Stockbridge School) remains a dynamic center of research and outreach.

62. Stockbridge Hall
James H. Ritchie, 1914

Bowker Auditorium
renovation: McClintock & Craig, 1954

Flint Laboratories
James H. Ritchie, 1912

Flint Laboratory and Stockbridge Hall were two of a set of three teaching and research buildings planned for construction between 1912 and 1914 along Olmsted Road (later Ellis Drive) to the west of Draper Hall (1903). The third building, to be dedicated to agricultural mechanics, was never built.

Work commenced on both Flint Laboratory and Stockbridge Hall in 1912, after Warren H. Manning (formerly affiliated with the Olmsted firm), labored for some four years over a comprehensive plan for the campus. W. H. Bowker, a member of the first graduating class and later a trustee of MAC, had pointed out that the lack of a comprehensive campus plan led to some less than ideal placements of buildings, calling the siting of Draper itself a "blunder." At the dedication of Stockbridge Hall, he would observe, "It was the unfortunate location of Draper Hall and the desire of one of our faculty to build a henhouse on the edge of campus that aroused [the Board] to the necessity of having a well-thought-out scheme of landscape treatment of the grounds."[1] Now the Trustees "considered it imperative for the college to plan harmonious development that would conserve the beauty of campus grounds while meeting the needs of a growing student population whose expanding range of activities was unprecedented."[2]

The architect of both Flint Laboratory and Stockbridge Hall, James H. Ritchie, was based in Boston; he had already designed French Hall (1909) and would in time return to offer plans for Memorial Hall (1921), Goessmann (1922), and other buildings as well.

Stockbridge Hall flanked by Flint Laboratory (left) and Draper Hall (right)

Flint Laboratory, detail

These early contributions suggest his priorities: advancing the Georgian Revival unfolding across campus. Flint Laboratory's original function as a dairy laboratory is signaled by the cow's head motif that Ritchie placed above the main entry; at the time of its completion (achieved at the same time as four new structures for the poultry program as well, and a sheep barn, in addition to the newly completed Grinnell Arena), the facility was considered to be "one of the best equipped dairy buildings in the United States," and the building described as "a model for the whole country." [3] Ritchie's Flint Laboratory was a two-story Georgian Revival brick building with a hip roof, an entry portico, and hip roof dormers on its south elevation. The building is three bays wide and nine bays deep, with a slate roof, stone trim, and a brick foundation. The trim includes a water table, string courses, monumental brick pilasters with simple stone capitals and bases, and dentil molding at the cornice.

Next door, massive pilasters flanking huge Corinthian columns announce the entrance to the much-larger and grander Stockbridge Hall. Built of brick and trimmed in limestone, the stately three-story Stockbridge Hall fronted a full 166 feet on the campus lawn before it, making a significant statement on the college landscape. While the broad brick facade confers a sense of permanence, interior walls on all three floors were planned in gypsum block, to facilitate radical changes in the arrangement of space, "provided future needs make changes necessary." [4] The building housed, in addition to facilities for agronomy, animal husbandry, farm administration and rural engineering, enterprises like the rural journalism program, a museum, and the department of agricultural education.

Bowker Auditorium

Inside Stockbridge Hall, an elegant auditorium—named in 1918 to honor alumnus William H. Bowker in recognition for his thirty-years service as a trustee—boasted a "beautiful organ" as well as a "motion-picture machine," necessary given the emerging technology's "growing use in educational work."[5] Bowker Auditorium quickly became a key gathering space on campus, including the annual fall faculty convocation and spring commencement. At the time it opened, it could seat the entire student body. Today it serves as an active music venue on campus, hosting musicians from Duke Ellington to U2.

63. Draper Hall
Emory A. Ellsworth, 1903

Built principally to serve as an improved dining hall, Draper Hall also sheltered the first dedicated dorm space for women on the MAC campus. The dining facilities occupied the main floor of the building, while female students were housed on the upper floors.

Women were part of the student population here from early in the campus' history, albeit in those early years a small one. Another nearby land-grant institution, Cornell University, had admitted its first female student in 1870; administrators at "Mass Aggie" did not want to be left behind as higher education in the United States expanded to serve women, but the lack of suitable campus housing had made it difficult to launch a meaningful program. Draper Hall made it possible to accommodate women in a special two-year course that balanced classes in subjects like soils, fertilizers, botany, chemistry, and zoology with instruction in greenhouse construction and management, propagation and pruning, and vegetable gardening, as well as French, German, and free-hand drawing. It would not be until the years surrounding World War I that women became a visible presence on campus, but the first graduate degree to be conferred on a woman was the 1905 master's degree achieved by Elizabeth High Smith; the first undergraduate degrees, awarded that same year, went to Esther Cowles Cushman (Entomology) and Monica Lillian Sanborn (Horticulture).

Draper Hall was designed by Emory A. Ellsworth, who had already contributed West Experiment Station in 1887, East Experiment Station in 1890, and Munson Hall in 1898. At this point in his career, Ellsworth billed himself as a "Rural Architect, Agricultural Engineer, and Landscape Gardner" (later he would emphasize his abilities in engineering). He had also given some thought to intersections between farm design and women's lives: James Elliot Read's guide *Farming for Profit* quotes Ellsworth as musing, "Need we wonder, when we consider the many useless, weary steps that must be taken, and the stock of vital strength that is continually wasted in the performance of household duties, that so many ambitious farmers wives are broken down in health and spirits at thirty five and must then remain for the rest of life the suffering victims of thoughtless careless interior household arrangement."[6] Presumably his design for Draper Hall reflected these sensibilities, but whatever choices were made in the interior arrangement of spaces, the exterior result is a light and airy building that evinces a certain gentility. Ellsworth's work on the three nineteenth-century buildings embraced Queen

Anne and Romanesque details, but Draper Hall's design (called simply "Colonial" at the time the building opened) is based on Georgian models, and also shows a Palladian influence (perhaps foreshadowing drawings for Munson Hall, still to come). One of its distinctive elements is the number of porticoes that project from the main block. The front door features a broad segmental arch with vertical sidelights to admit light, an element repeated in upper-story balconies, and which also gestures toward elite residential architecture in the Colonial Revival style.

In the 1910s and '20s, Draper Hall was the focal point of women's lives on campus. In time, the creation of a quadrangle of dorms along North Pleasant Street altered the center of gravity for women on campus, but Draper Hall remained a key dining hall on campus until Worcester Dining Commons was added in 1953 in response to a growing student population.

64. Goessmann Laboratory
James H. Ritchie, 1922

In the wake of World War I, university administrators began developing comprehensive five- and ten-year plans that integrated curricular needs with the physical plant. In these years, the agricultural experiment station was expanded, the Brooks tobacco barn and associated farmland were acquired, new laboratories were built, and new common spaces created, including Memorial Hall.

Goessmann Laboratory, just east of Draper Hall, was part of this broader development. The original chemistry building, erected in 1869 near the present site of Machmer Hall, had been the institutional home of the school's first chemist, Charles A. Goessmann, but a half century later it had fallen into disrepair. In 1922, a fire broke out in the old building. Professors Charles Peters and Joseph Chamberlain managed to break into the basement to rescue a new order of chemistry supplies and, with the assistance of firemen, saved much of the contents of the library by throwing books out of a window onto a lab coat. But the building was ultimately destroyed.

Luckily, work was already under way toward a successor. By this date, the chemistry program was scattered across campus, in the Flint Laboratory, West Experiment Station, South College, and other buildings. The new lab would bring MAC's chemists together in a dedicated space.

The building would be named for Goessmann, a German scientist who began his career in theoretical chemistry, though it was his work in applied chemistry—and particularly sugar beets, sugar cane, sorghum, and salt manufacture—that secured his international reputation. Goessmann arrived in the United States in 1857 and after several years at the Rensselaer Polytechnic Institute moved to Amherst in 1868, establishing the Chemistry Department as well as a program of research and experimentation on agricultural chemistry. He was instrumental in the reclamation of Massachusetts's salt marshes and transformed the fertilizer industry in the Commonwealth.

When this building arose a just over a decade after Goessman's death in 1910, it was clear that the structure would be named in his honor. Architecturally, the building

Draper Hall

was also part of Georgian Revival on campus. Built of reinforced concrete, its red brick exterior is contrasted by artificial stone. Its design is not quite symmetrical, with the east wing extending twenty one feet longer than the west. In design it is fairly restrained, its most notable ornamentation being the smooth stone sheathing, fully two stories in height, that marks the building's entrance; a segmental pediment supported by rusticated Ionic pilasters surrounds the recessed doorway. An especially notable feature of the Goessmann Chemistry Laboratory is the way in which it displays a genealogy of the field of chemistry as it had shaped and was then shaping the campus. As UMass Chemistry professor David L. Adams has explained, the seven names inscribed on the upper facade of the building—Liebig, Boussingault, Wohler, Johnson, Lawes, Gilbert and Hilgarde—honor pioneers in agricultural chemistry:

> Justus von Liebig, the "Father of Agricultural Chemistry", discovered that crops took up their mineral matter from the soil and first suggested use of fertilizers. He was the first to use laboratory instruction in chemical education. Boussingault was a noted French agricultural chemist who made progress in understanding the assimilation of nitrogen by plants, and who conducted the first agricultural field experiments. Friedrich Wohler, who synthesized the first organic compound from non-living materials, was Goessmann's teacher. Samuel W. Johnson instituted the first fertilizer inspection in the United States. In 1875 he founded and directed the Connecticut Experiment Station, the first in the United States. The Englishmen Sir John Lawes and J. H. Gilbert established the first experiment station at Rothamsted, England, where they researched problems of animal nutrition. Hilgarde was a noted authority on soil chemistry and director of the California Experiment Station.[7]

"Today," Adams continues, "these names stand in silent testimony to an era when chemistry made its most important contributions to agriculture, food, and nutrition."[8]

Goessmann Laboratory

This stained glass memorial window was given in 1907 on the occasion of Charles Goessmann's eightieth birthday.

In addition to lab and classroom space, the central portion of the building, in the basement and ground floor, contains a 165-seat auditorium. The second floor once housed the chemistry library, including main room, a seminar room, and the "Goessmann Memorial Alcove" in which was displayed some of the professor's books and apparatus.

Lighting the space is a 42-by-36-inch stained glass memorial window, given in 1907 on the occasion of Goessmann's 80th birthday. The window originally hung in Goessmann's office, but now greets visitors in the lobby of the building. The upper left corner features a shield with the symbols of Fulda, Fritzlar, and Gottingen (Goessmann having trained at the University of Gottingen). The shield of the University of Gottingen features Minerva, the goddess of wisdom. The circular image at the bottom of the frame show the tools of the chemist: a glass retort, blowpipe assayer's tongs, a Hessian crucible (that is, a ceramic container designed to withstand high heat), and test tubes, all surrounded by flame. The floral decoration includes wisteria but also foliage of the peanut plant, another object of Goessmann's research.

In the 1950s, the expansive growth of the sciences across campus created a need for more space, so the present-day annex was erected near the end of that decade.

65. John W. Lederle Graduate Research Center
Campbell, Aldrich & Nulty, 1966

In December 1962, the President's Science Advisory Committee issued an urgent call for action in the engineering, mathematical and physical sciences. Demands in "defense, space, and foreign assistance" meant that the "nation must take immediate steps to enhance its utilization and supply of manpower in all fields of science and technology." Among recommendations to dramatically increase the number of students training in these fields, the report also called for the "strengthening of existing centers of excellence" in these fields.[9] The UMass Graduate Research Center was proposed to advance that aim.

Later named in honor of John W. Lederle (UMass president from 1960 to 1970), the Graduate Research Center's designs were submitted in 1964, and the building began rising in 1966. Intended from the outset to be the "focal center of the north end of campus," planners asserted that "architectural distinction is therefore required";

John W. Lederle Graduate Research Center

Since the building "will be visited and used by important people...the university's public image is at stake."[10] Initially envisioned as three high-rise buildings and three low-rise buildings, plans were eventually scaled back to include one low-rise and three attached high-rise buildings.

Scott Quinlan of Campbell, Aldrich & Nulty—the lead architect on this project—had originally envisioned the seventeen-story building in limestone, following his design of the recently completed library at Tufts University, where he had enjoyed working with the material. Cost constraints and regulations from the Division of Capital Planning at the state level required a compromise, however. Precast concrete for the facade proved an acceptable alternative. The material was finer and denser than poured concrete and created a more polished final appearance (initially the concrete was left in its natural finish, but it has since been painted a warmer off-white color).

Quinlan was inspired by New York City's Lever House (1962), designed by Gordon Bunshaft of Skidmore, Owings & Merrill (sometimes identified as the architect of the McGuirk Alumni Stadium). The fenestration is influenced by the function of the spaces they contain. For instance, library windows on the low-rise have full windows to allow natural light to permeate the space, while individual offices and labs in the towers required smaller windows.

Ventilation was also an important feature of the design. Laboratories needed separate systems so that potentially volatile fumes would not mix in communal air vents. A ventilation shaft runs along the south elevation of the towers, with an articulated elbow emerging at the top. Quinlan later recalled that he had been inspired by the design of a Dunhill cigarette lighter that he was using at the time, though it also seemed to anticipate the Pompidou Center by Richard Rodgers and Renzo Piano (1977), which pioneered a late modernist motif of bringing the infrastructure of buildings, such as stairs and pipes, to the exterior facade. The building also required 100 percent humidity control to prevent warping of the punch cards that contained data for the computers at the time.

The design for the Graduate Research Tower led to other contracts for the firm. Campbell, Aldrich & Nulty also designed Whitmore Hall and the School of Management Building, and would return to Amherst to design Amherst College's Merrill Science Center (1968)—the latter contract for another campus science facility in part due to the successful UMass project. The following year the firm contributed to the creation of Boston's landmark City Hall (1969, with Kallmann, McKinnell & Knowles) and First National Bank Building (1971).

Silvio O. Conte National Center for Polymer Research

66. Silvio O. Conte National Center for Polymer Research
Janet Ross of Ellenzweig Associates with Whitney Atwood Norcross Associates, 1996

Named for U.S. Congressman Silvio O. Conte of Pittsfield, Massachusetts, who championed polymer research and helped secure funding for the center, this building when finished was the nation's largest and most modern polymer research facility.

Architect Janet Ross of Ellenzweig Associates conceived the glass and granite building that houses the Silvio O. Conte National Center for Polymer Research as two distinct wings, one housing offices and the other laboratories. Founded in Cambridge in 1965 and closely connected to both the Massachusetts Institute of Technology and Harvard University, Ellenzweig Associates had long established itself in the field of technically-demanding designs for science research facilities when it was engaged to create the Conte Center. Ross proposed a north-facing six-story office wing faced with an enameled steel and glass curtain wall. An arcade of exposed steel beams and stone-clad pillars serves no structural function but creates an inviting entranceway to the building. The curved design of the office wing draws the eye into a courtyard created by the convergence of the Center and the Graduate Research Towers. The eight-story laboratory wing has limestone paneling and a granite base that blends with other buildings in the immediate vicinity. Tucked between the limestone, glass, and granite stands a small garden of nine trees and assorted plantings with benches for an out-of-the-way gathering space.

Computer Science Research Center

67. Computer Science Research Center
Whitney Atwood Norcross Associates, 1999

This modern building houses the current day computer science facility with state-of-the-art amenities, but computer science at UMass had much humbler beginnings. Computer research first came to UMass in the early 1960s as an accessory to the needs of the chemistry department. It eventually was awarded its own program as the Research Computing Center. By 1964, the University Trustees had approved a Master of Science graduate degree, and a PhD program was approved in 1972, the same year that the department moved into the Lederle Graduate Research Center, where it remained until it moved to its own building in 1999.

The department has long demonstrated strengths in machine learning, informational retrieval, software engineering, and theoretical computer science, and continues to develop new fields like graphics, security and privacy, and digital forensics.

The Computer Science Building proudly displays its structural elements as part of its external design. The exterior features the exposed bracing that makes up the skeletal structure of the building, designed to hold up against wind stress. Offices are placed along exterior walls in order to maximize access to natural light.

68. Engineering Research Building
Ellenzweig Associates and Whitney Atwood Norcross Associates, 2004

This 57,000-square-foot facility—designed by Ellenzweig Associates, a follow-up to their successful plans for the Conte Center in the mid-1990s—was built to house portions of the Civil and Environmental Engineering and Chemical Engineering departments, the graduate Environmental Program's research labs, and a geo-environmental research lab. The three-story brick block contains labs; across a lobby lit by skylights—"an architectural thoroughfare for the campus," leading to parking facilities below—is a two-story circular volume that houses a Learning Center, including a 195-seat lecture

Engineering Research Building

hall and a thirty-five-seat distance learning classroom.[11] In a move that gestures back to the gypsum block employed in the construction of Stockbridge Hall to facilitate future renovations, "all of the building's laboratory areas are based on flexible planning modules, allowing the building to be configured into single- and multiple-module laboratories; typical floors were designed to accommodate future reconfiguration."[12] Meanwhile, the exterior materials—red brick, metal, and glass—aim to integrate the building into its context. The Learning Center, for instance, is clad in scored metal sheathing that feels contemporary while simultaneously suggesting rustication.

RDK Engineers consulted on this project and later contributed as well to the Integrated Sciences building. University officials presented the engineers with some design challenges to address; in particular, they laudably hoped to keep any equipment off of the roof of the auditorium in order to preserve scenic views from other, taller buildings. To accommodate this request, RDK housed their ventilation systems in the basement and ran air through the crawl space, under the atrium, and into the auditorium.

69. Gunness Engineering Laboratory
Appleton & Stearns, 1948

Electrical Engineering Wing
1950

Gunness Engineering Laboratory, named in honor of Christian I. Gunness, professor of rural engineering at MAC (and a man who "took up the task of developing courses in machinery and structures at a time when technology was rendering obsolete much of the equipment to be found on New England farms"), was built in 1948 on the former agricultural fields north of Draper Hall. [13] It aimed to serve the newly formed school of engineering, and houses space for civil, mechanical, and electrical engineering and their many majors.

Gunness Laboratory, humble though it may appear, was designed by the celebrated firm of Appleton & Stearns, known as Peabody & Stearns until 1919 when W. Cornell Appleton and Frank A. Stearns formed their own enterprise following Peabody's 1917 death. Appleton was the last chief designer for Peabody & Stearns, which designed the original Breakers (1895) in Newport, Rhode Island; City Hall in Worcester, Massachusetts (1898); and the Custom House Tower (1915) in Boston, among many other projects. They were one of the most prominent architectural firms of the late nineteenth and early twentieth centuries and helped usher in nationwide neoclassical revival. Following this trend, which had made its way to UMass, Appleton and Stearns designed a streamlined Georgian Revival building. The architecturally modest building would be joined, in quick succession, by Marston Hall (1950) and Paige Laboratory (1950), and in time by the Animal Isolation Laboratory (1953) and Thayer Animal Disease Laboratory (1957), filling in these farmlands with new facilities dedicated to the advancement of scientific research.

The building helps map the long trajectory of engineering at UMass. When Gunness first began teaching courses on farm structures and machinery, in 1915 in the newly built Stockbridge Hall, the college was yet a latecomer to the field; at that date, MAC's commitment to engineering did not extend beyond surveying and bridge and road construction—skills farmers clearly needed. With his courses and research, Gunness helped usher in a new era. In the 1930s and '40s, World War II would serve as a catalyst to those aims, and the new lab—together with Hasbrouck Laboratory on North Pleasant Street and other facilities around campus—would advance the field on campus and beyond while (administrators hoped) addressing the more pressing issues that had arrived with the nuclear age. At the building's 1949 dedication, Massachusetts Governor Paul A. Dever asserted that the "only solace of the world in this time of atomic implications is in the balanced training and sober common sense of a free citizenry."[14]

Marston Hall

70. Marston Hall
Appleton & Stearns, 1949 and 1954

Having contributed the design of Gunness Laboratory, it was no surprise when Appleton & Stearns returned to campus to plan Marston Hall. Constructed in two phases, this huge three-story symmetrical composition extends under a flat roof with a low parapet wall. The nine-bay central block contains the building's entrance, at the midpoint, between two opposing towers.

East and west wings define a rear courtyard. Machine-made brick, laid in a common-bond pattern from foundation to parapet, create a sense of stability. A continuous limestone belt course defines the ground floor. The comparatively utilitarian windows have flat brick arches and limestone sills. Brick quoins ornament the corners of the exterior of the building and the three wings are unified by a narrow limestone frieze and cornice.

The functional appearance of most of Marston Hall is enlivened somewhat at the central bay, which projects from the facade and is faced with limestone at the base and limestone quoins integrated with brick veneer at the upper levels. Limestone pilasters and a classical entablature with a dentil cornice frame the doorway, through which visitors find wooden double French doors with divided lights and a transom divided by a decorative arched colonnade. The recessed entrance vestibule faced with limestone veneer provides a certain warmth absent from the otherwise severe expanse of brick. The frontispiece continues above the entrance entablature with a stone-carved building plaque and a swan's neck surround, the whole terminated by the upper window bay and bracketed stone window case.

The building is named for Professor George A. Marston, named the first dean of the newly instituted College of Engineering when the Trustees created it in 1947; he would serve until 1963, overseeing the explosive growth of the College in its first years. In addition to the wide range of services the building provided engineering students and faculty, the campus radio station, WMUA (still managed today by university students), was originally located on the ground floor of the 1954 wing, remaining there for nearly thirty years before moving, in 1983, to the Lincoln Campus Center.

71. Andrew C. Knowles III Engineering Building
Cambridge Seven Associates, 1991

Parallel to Marston Hall with its east end adjacent to Marcus Hall, the Andrew C. Knowles III Engineering Building is a 24,000-square-foot brick structure constructed to complement existing buildings and create an Engineering Quadrangle. The building

Andrew C. Knowles III Engineering Building

is one of Cambridge Seven's many structures on campus. Known for such dramatic buildings as the New England Aquarium in Boston (1967) and the 1985 Naismith Memorial Basketball Hall of Fame (the current building, dedicated in 2002, was designed by Gwathmey Siegel Associates of New York) in Springfield, here the firm produced a more muted building designed to fit in with its neighbors. The horizontal brick mass of the building is only interrupted by turquoise and red brick banding, tying it to Marcus Hall to the east.

The research facility was built to enhance and augment the research activities of the College of Engineering. "What it is all about are the kids we are going to educate," said 1957 electrical engineering graduate Andrew Knowles (who had chaired the college's capital campaign), "the graduate students—people who will pass through here like I did through Marston Hall."[15]

72. Marcus Hall and the Gunness Engineering Student Center
Drummey Rosane Anderson, 1966

Student Center Addition
Kuhn Riddle Architects, 1985

Originally known simply as Engineering Building East and renamed in 1985 to honor retired professor Joseph S. Marcus, Marcus Hall contains a 300-seat auditorium, a fluid mechanics lab, and a 160-mph wind tunnel. At the time of the building's construction, the UMass School of Engineering was second in size among the university's schools and colleges, with 900 undergraduates, 125 graduate students, and 60 faculty members. The 1966 building was designed by Drummey Rosane Anderson (DRA) of Boston.

Four decades later the building was expanded with the addition of the Gunness Engineering Student Center. The Student Union at the center of campus was proving increasingly inconvenient for engineering students, who needed space nearer to

Marcus Hall and the Gunness Engineering Student Center

their classrooms and labs in which to "study, collaborate on assignments, relax, and socialize."[16] The addition "includes an impressive entryway called the Marcus Atrium that stretches from a curved stairway to the top of metal-capped peak at the head of the Engineering Quadrangle." The design, created by the Amherst architectural firm Kuhn Riddle, included plans not only for the building itself but also for the landscaping of the entire quadrangle. The resulting building provides a reception area for visiting lecturers and corporate recruiters, as well as meeting space for student activities and professional societies. The designers believed that one of the most significant roles of the center was to "facilitate social exchange among students leading to lifelong friendships.... We are certain that this new center will serve this most important function and will kindle friendships, togetherness, and a spirit of shared achievement among our engineering students."[17]

1 Dedication of Stockbridge Hall, Stockbridge Hall, Buildings and Grounds, RG-3, SCUA.

2 W. Maros, C. Weed, and C. Beagan, Massachusetts Historical Commission, AMH.103, May 2009.

3 Porter E. Sargent, ed., A Handbook of New England, 2nd ed. (Boston: George H. Ellis Company, 1917), 342; and Federal Writers' Project of the Works Progress Administration of Massachusetts, Massachusetts: A Guide to Its Places and People (Boston: Riverside Press, Houghton Mifflin, 1937), 127. On the poultry program and other facilities see Massachusetts Agricultural College Catalogue, 1912–13 5 (Boston: Wright and Potter, 1913), 6.

4 Massachusetts Agricultural College Catalogue, 1912–13 8 (Boston: Wright and Potter, 1916), 21.

5 Ibid.

6 James E. Read, Farming for Profit: An Encyclopedia of Useful Information and a Practical Assistant in the Management of Farm Affairs (Philadelphia: J. C. McCurdy & Co., 1884), 81.

7 David L. Adams, "Brief History of the Department of Chemistry at the University of Massachusetts at Amherst," typescript, July 1998, 19, SCUA.

8 Ibid.

9 President's Science Advisory Committee, "Meeting Manpower Needs in Science and Technology" (December 1962), SCUA.

10 Lederle Graduate Research Tower, Buildings and Grounds, RG-36, SCUA.

11 See the University of Massachusetts Engineering Research Building on the architect's website, http://www.ellenzweig.com.

12 Ibid.

13 Harold Whiting Cary, The University of Massachusetts: A History of One Hundred Years (Amherst: University of Massachusetts Press, 1962), 107.

14 "Dever Present at Dedication of Gunness Lab Saturday," Collegian, October 27, 1949, Group 36, Series 101, Box 8, Folder 1 "Gunness Lab 1947, 1949," SCUA.

15 "Knowles Dedication a Bright Day for Engineering," http://engineering.umass.edu/collegehistory/knowles-dedication-bright-day-for-engineering

16 "New Student Center to Crown Engineering Quad," Campus Chronicle, August 10, 1990, Group 36, Series 101, Box 11, Folder "Marcus Hall (1955–)," SCUA.

17 Ibid.

Acknowledgments

In writing this guidebook we have accumulated debts faster than buildings went up at UMass in the 1960s. First, we would like to thank those keepers of the history of UMass. First and foremost is Joseph Larson, professor emeritus and a founder, together with Richard Nathhorst, of Preserve UMass; his encyclopedic knowledge of the campus is only matched by his passionate advocacy for preserving our history. We received enormous assistance as well from Richard Nathhorst, Rob Cox, and Arnold Friedman. We have relied on their research, words, and advice. Their influence is on virtually every page.

Our eagerness to celebrate the modern architecture of the campus received a major boost at the 2007 conference on midcentury modernism that brought key architects and scholars of that era to campus to give new attention to UMass's valuable outdoor exhibition of midcentury buildings.

Over the years we have set a number of students researching UMass's architectural history, including Jayne Bernhard-Armington, Jessica Frankenfield, Izzy Kornblatt, Kirin Makker, Katrina Spade, and Lawsin Wulsin in particular, who all contributed valuable research to this project. For their willingness to sit for interviews we are deeply grateful to UMass assistant director of Facilities and Campus Planning John Mathews (who is to be doubly thanked for his careful reading of the draft) architects Kevin Roche, Bruce Thomas and R. Scott Quinlan, Ron Ostberg, Sigrid Miller Pollin, and Ray Mann. Our faculty and staff colleagues David Glassberg, Bob Paynter, Marty Smith, Dennis Swinford, Tim Rohan, Theodore Djaferis, John Mathews, Pat Parenteau, and David Adams all generously fielded queries and read pages of the draft. Amy Glynn, Steve Robbins, Anne Moore, Shaowei Wang, John Solem, Danielle Kovacs, and Jon Haeber offered valuable assistance with images. Public history student Jaimie Squardo Kicklighter supplied essential administrative support as the project reached its final stages. Todd Diacon, then-deputy chancellor of UMass Amherst, believed in this project from the outset; we are grateful to him for his enthusiastic embrace of this campus and this project.

I would especially like to thank my father, Alex Page, who taught at UMass for thirty years and introduced me to an appreciation of architecture, and to Eve and our children, Jonah, Aviva, and Ruthie, who have spent their fair share of time on the campus—Eve as the head of the Labor Center and our children as regular visitors to the Fine Arts Center. I hope they all will have a renewed appreciation of our campus, and architecture around the world we will see in our travels together.
—*Max Page*

Let me add my thanks to my students, who continually help me appreciate the campus in new ways, and to my husband, Steve Peck, for his unending support for this project and for many other labors of love.
—*Marla Miller*

Bibliography

MAPS AND VISUAL EVIDENCE

Anonymous. "Estate of the Mass. Agricultural College," Amherst, 1870.

Anonymous. Map of the Mass Aglr. Col. Student's Handbook, 1893–1894.

Anonymous. Map of MAC and Environs, Col. Student's Handbook, 1893–1894; 1911.

Anonymous. MAC campus, Student's Handbook, 1926.

Anonymous. "Campus Guide for Visitors, University of Massachusetts, Amherst, Massachusetts," including a plan, "University of Massachusetts, Amherst, Massachusetts." Special Collections and Archives (SCUA), 1955.

Anonymous. 1966–67 Student Handbook.

Anonymous. 1968 Student Handbook.

Anonymous. Oblique aerial photograph of the campus looking north, 1970s. SCUA.

Anonymous. C. 1975. Oblique aerial photograph of the campus looking northwest, SCUA.

Armstrong, William H. "Guide Map of the Campus" (based on A. K. Harrison) in *Campus Guide, Massachusetts State College, Amherst, Mass.* 1939.

———. "Guide Map of the Campus" in *Campus Guide, Massachusetts State College, Amherst, Mass.* 1943.

———. "Guide Map of the Campus" in *Campus Guide, University of Massachusetts, Amherst, Mass.* 1948–49.

Beers, F. W., "Amherst." 1873.

Burleigh, L. R., "Amherst, Mass., 1886." (lithograph). 1886.

"Competition…University of Minnesota Campus" (James H. Ritchie and Warren H. Manning) Architectural Review 15 (1908), 132.

Darling, E. S. "A Plan of the Town of Amherst 1830." Massachusetts Archives.

Gray, Alonzo, and Charles B. Adams. "A Map of Amherst, with a view of the College and Mount Pleasant Institution." 1833.

Harrison, A. K., Massachusetts Agricultural Campus, Student Handbook, 1913.

———. "Massachusetts State College." 1935.

———. "Massachusetts State College," Visitor's Guide to Massachusetts State College, 1937.

Manganaro, Anthony J. "University of Massachusetts, Guide Map of the Campus." 1947.

———. "Campus Map: University of Massachusetts at Amherst." 1956.

Manning, Warren H. "Massachusetts Agricultural College, Amherst, Mass, General Plan. September 1910."

Waugh, Frank A. "Massachusetts Agricultural College, Amherst, Mass, General Plan. January 1920."

UMASS PUBLICATIONS

Alumni Bulletin, 1922–1931 [Massachusetts Agricultural College]; 1931–41 [Massachusetts State College].

Index, the school yearbook, published 1839–1931 [Massachusetts Agricultural College]; 1932–47 [Massachusetts State College]; and University of Massachusetts, 1948–2005.

Massachusetts Agricultural College annual reports, 1864–1932.

Buildings and Grounds, RG-36.

Faculty Senate Committees: Campus Beautification, RG-40.

Dean of Women Helen Curtis Cole Papers, 1902–1993, RG-30.

Oswald Tippo Papers, FS 106.

President's Office, RG-3.

Ruth J. Totman Papers, FS 097.

UNPUBLISHED SOURCES

Adams, David L. "The G Chem Lab." Typescript, 1997, SCUA.

Adams, David L. "Brief History of the Department of Chemistry at the University of Massachusetts at Amherst." Typescript, July 1998.

Arrigo, Matthew. "The Orchard Hill Observatory." Typescript, May 2007 (Paynter Collection).

Brown, Hannah. "The Archaeology of Butterfield Hall." Typescript, May 2010 (Paynter Collection).

Duffey, Joseph. "A Tribute to Ruth Totman." -SCUA FS 97 Box 2 Folder 14.

Fixler, David, for Einhorn Yaffee Prescott. University of Massachusetts Amherst Historic Building Inventory: Final Survey Report, 2009.

Joseph R. Rogers Jr. Swimming Pool Dedication Brochure, April 26, 1986, SCUA RG36/101/Boyden.

Keith, Vicky. "Mass Aggie Women, 1910–23." Typescript, 1983.

Noonan, Mark. "History of Rhododendron Garden." Typescript, for Rhododendron Garden Renovation Project Committee, SCUA.

O'Brien, Timothy. "You Can't Get There From Here Anymore: A Partial History of Stockbridge Road, Amherst, Massachusetts." Typescript, 2010 (Paynter Collection).

O'Donnell, Robert. "Undergraduate Women and the Post-War College: The University of Massachusetts." Typescript, 1996.

Shurcliff, Shurcliff & Merrill, Landscape Architects, and Neils H. Larsen, Architectural Consultant. "University of Massachusetts, Amherst, Massachusetts, Master Plan, Prepared for the Division of Building Construction," June 1957.

Stillman, Sheron. "A History of the Department of Physical Education for Women at the University of Massachusetts 1917–65," WPE 86-Seminar, January 1965, UMass SCUA RG25 P3/2.

University of Massachusetts. Legacy Buildings: Analysis and Strategic Choices. March, 2007.

University of Massachusetts. "Massachusetts State College Report from Alumni Advisory Committee on Campus Development" (Alumni Committee 1945:7).

PUBLISHED SOURCES

"Drill Hall Razed to Make Way for Liberal Arts Building." *Massachusetts Alumnus* (Summer 1958).

"Hard Times Bring Greatest Rush of Students to State College," *Boston Globe*, October 5, 1930.

"Planning of the 1980s," n.d., http://www.umass.edu/afroam/planning.html.

"Science Building Opens Doors," *Collegian* (February 2, 2009).

"The 20 Ugliest Colleges in the USA." Campus Squeeze. http://www.campussqueeze.com/post/The-20-Ugliest-Colleges-in-the-USA.aspx. December 4, 2009.

"UMass Mapping Plans to Expand Athletics," *Boston Daily Record*, March 28, 1967: SCUA RG 18/2.

Abrahamson, Michael. "Brutalism: The Word Itself and What We Mean When We Say It." Critic Under the Influence (blog). http://criticundertheinfluence.wordpress.com (November 20, 2011).

Adams, David L., and Lynne E. Adams. Massachusetts Memories: UMass Amherst History. Amherst: Collective Copies, 2008.

Almeida, João Pedro. *The Frank A. Waugh Arboretum: Challenges and Opportunities on An Evolving Landscape*. Amherst: University of Massachusetts Amherst, 2005.

Barnhart, Benjamin. "Up-to-the-Minuteman," *UMass Magazine* (Spring 2002).

Becker, Kerstin. *Through These Doors: The History of the University of Massachusetts Minuteman Marching Band*. Amherst: Old Chapel Press, 2004.

Bergquist, Richard E. "The Frank L. Boyden Physical Education Building," *Massachusetts Alumnus* (Winter 1965/66).

de Botton, Alain. *Architecture of Happiness*. New York: Pantheon, 2006.

Bradlee, Ben. "More defects in buildings at UMass" *Boston Globe* (September 7, 1979).

Brown, Emma. "John Carl Warnecke dies at 91, designed Kennedy gravesite," *Washington Post* (April 23, 2010).

Caldwell, Jean. "Brick chips are falling at $16.8m UMass library," *Boston Globe* (December 8, 1976).

Campbell, Robert. "A Prototype, but Never to Be Repeated," *Boston Globe* (January 6, 1974).

Carpenter, Edward Wilton, and Charles Frederick Morehouse. *The History of the Town of Amherst, Massachusetts*. Amherst: Press of Carpenter & Morehouse, 1896.

Cary, Harold Whiting. *University of Massachusetts: A History of 100 Years*. Amherst: University of Massachusetts Press, 1962.

Caswell, L. B. *Brief History of the Massachusetts Agricultural College*. Springfield, Mass.: 1917.

Clausen, Meredith L. Pietro Belluschi: Modern American Architect. Cambridge, Mass.: MIT Press, 1999.

Davies, Hugh Marlais. Artist & Fabricator: Exhibition Held at the Fine Arts Center Gallery, University of Massachusetts/Amherst, September 23–November 9, 1975. Amherst: Fine Arts Center Gallery, University of Massachusetts, 1975.

Dempsey, David K., and Raymond P. Baldwin. *The Triumphs and Trials of Lotta Crabtree*. New York: Morrow, 1968.

Federal Writers' Project of the Works Progress Administration of Massachusetts. *Massachusetts: A Guide to Its Places and People*. Boston: Riverside Press, 1937.

Fitzgibbons, Daniel J. "Arnold House Turns 50," *In the Loop: News for Staff & Faculty*. 2004.

Freeland, Richard M. *America's Golden Age: Universities in Massachusetts, 1945–70*. New York: Oxford University Press, 1992.

Friedman, Arnold. *Three Architectural Tours: Selected Buildings on the Campus of the University of Massachusetts Amherst*. Amherst: University of Massachusetts Campus Beautification Committee, 2000.

Fuess, Claude M. *Amherst, The Story of a New England College*. Boston, 1935.

Gyure, Dale Allen. "The Heart of the University: A History of the Library as an Architectural Symbol of American Higher Education," *Winterthur Portfolio* 42, 2/3 (2008): 107–24.

Hassan, Samuel. "Sylvan Area: Living 'the suite life.'" *Massachusetts Daily Collegian*. (May 1, 1974).

Horowitz, Helen Lefkowitz. *Alma Mater: Design and Experience in the Women's Colleges from their Nineteenth Century Beginnings to the 1930s*. New York: Alfred Knopf, 1984.

Judd, Sylvester. *History of Hadley Including the Early History of Hatfield, South Hadley, Amherst and Granby, Massachusetts*. Springfield, Mass.: H. R. Huntting & Co., 1905.

Karson, Robin. "Warren H. Manning: Pragmatist in the Wild Garden," *Nature and Ideology: Natural Garden Design in the Twentieth Century*, ed. Joachim Wolschke-Bulmahn. Washington, D.C.: Dumbarton Oaks Research Library and Collection, 1997.

Kidder, Tracy. *House*. Boston: Houghton Mifflin, 1985.

Klenotic, Deborah. "Building boom! At the future North Residential Area, cranes swing the campus into 'New Dirt' era." Advancement Communications, October 18, 2005.

Lounsbury, Carl R. "Beaux-Arts Ideals and Colonial Reality: The Reconstruction of Williamsburg's Capitol, 1928–34." *Journal of the Society of Architectural Historians* 49, no. 4 (December 1990): 373–89.

Lyons, Louis. "An Alumnus Looks Back 50 Years." *Boston Globe* (April 28, 1963).

Manning, Warren H. "The Autobiography of Warren H. Manning." Library of American Landscape History, 1937. Typescript.

Matsuda, Thomas, Searching for the Buddha in the Mountains. Thesis (MFA) University of Massachusetts Amherst, 1999.

McNamara, Eileen. "Why the Students Call It 'ZooMass': Falling Bricks, Leaking Roofs and Crime Plague Amherst Campus." *Boston Globe* (November 18, 1979).

Miller, Amelia F. *Connecticut River Valley Doorways: An Eighteenth-Century Flowering*. Boston: Boston University for the Dublin Seminar for New England Folklife, 1983.

Miller, Marla R. *Cultivating a Past: Essays on the History of Hadley, Massachusetts*. Amherst: University of Massachusetts Press, 2009.

Norton, Paul F. *Amherst: A Guide to Its Architecture*. Amherst: Amherst Historical Society, 1975.

Olmsted, Frederick Law. "A Few Things to be Thought of before Proceeding to Plan Buildings for the National Agricultural Colleges." In *The Papers of Fredrick Law Olmsted*. New York: American News Company, 1866.

Polumbaum, Ian. "20 Years Later, Memories of Life before Southwest," *Massachusetts Daily Collegian*, May 1, 1984.

Rand, Frank Prentice. *The Village of Amherst: A Landmark of Light*. Amherst: Amherst Historical Society, 1958.

———. Yesterdays at Massachusetts Agricultural College. Amherst: Associate Alumni, 1933.

Read, James Elliot. *Farming for Profit: A HandBook for the American Farmer*. Philadelphia, Penn.: J. C. McCurdy & Co., 1881.

Reck, Franklin M. *The 4-H Story: A History of 4-H Club Work*. Chicago: National Committee on Boys and Girls Club Work; Ames, Iowa: Iowa State College Press, 1951.

Ritchie, James H. "Eastern States Agricultural and Exhibition Group," *Architectural Forum* 27, no. 4 (1917): 99–104.

Rugen, Karen. "More than a House of Books," *American Libraries* 2, no. 8 (September 1971): 876–81.

Sargent, Porter E., ed. *A Handbook of New England*, 2nd ed. Boston: George H. Ellis Company, 1917.

Seidman, Irving. *Oswald Tippo and the Early Promise of the University of Massachusetts*. Amherst: Friends of the Library, 2002.

Shanor, Rick. "Giving Nature a Boost," *Boston Globe*, June 2, 1968.

Sippel, John. "Ain't No Stoppin' Us Now." *UMass Amherst* (Fall 2010): 18.

Smith, Andy. "Papers stunt UM complex," *Collegian*, November 29, 2007.

Story, Ronald, ed. *Five Colleges, Five Histories*. Amherst: University of Massachusetts Press, 1992.

Sullivan, Steven R. *University of Massachusetts Amherst*. Mount Pleasant, S.C.: Arcadia Press, 2004.

Thayer, Charles H. *History of Stockbridge House at Massachusetts State College*. Amherst: 1936.

Tolles, Bryant F. *Architecture & Academe: College Buildings in New England Before 1860*.

Totman, Conrad. *Recollections of Ruth Jane Totman*.

Turner, Paul Venable. *Campus: An American Planning Tradition*. Cambridge, Mass.: MIT Press, 1984.

Vickery, Margaret Birney. *Smith College*. New York: Princeton Architectural Press, 2007.

Wall, Bill. "Plant Conversion plans researched," *Collegian* (November 13, 1981).

Waugh, Frank. *Book of Landscape Gardening*, 1899 Reprinted by University of Massachusetts Press, 2006, Linda Flint McClelland, ed.

Wells, Ward Dyer, and John G. McGowan, "Design and Installation of Heating System for UMass Solar Habitat I," *Wind Energy Center Reports*, paper 25 (1976).

Wilson, Cheryl. "Beyond ivy, new landscapes greet returning students," *Hampshire Gazette* (September 10, 2004).

Wright, Patricia. "A Complex Edifice: Campus Skyscrapers Create Controversy," *Contact* 12, no. 2 (Winter 1987): 15–19.

WEBSITES

On Massachusetts 4-H History, see www.mass4h.org

On the Sunwheel, see http://donald.astro.umass.edu/~young/sunwheel/paper.html

On the UMass orchard, see http://www.coldspringorchard.com

On the Connecticut River, see http://water.epa.gov/type/watersheds/named/heritage

On UMass buildings, see http://www.library.umass.edu/spcoll/youmass/doku.php

Illustration Credits

All photography by Bilyena Dímitrova except the following:
John Solem: 14–15, 30, 43, 51, 58, 68, 74, 77, 95, 146, 170, 171
John Haeber: 45, 108, 109, 131 (bottom)
Alex Page: 11

All black-and-white archival photography used courtesy of SCUA;
also color images on 27, 41, 112, and 123.

Index